INDEX / TABLE OF CONTENTS

THE SUBLIME ENCYCLOPEDIA BY NATHAN COPPEDGE

| [Impossible magic could be possible again.] |

THE SUBLIME

ENCYCLOPEDIA

A HISTORY OF HISTORY'S GREATEST IDEAS

BY NATHAN COPPEDGE

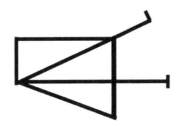

THE SUBLIME ENCYCLOPEDIA BY NATHAN COPPEDGE

\INTRO\

This text collects some of the most important writings of Nathan Larkin Coppedge: Philosopher, Artist, Inventor, Poet, who was born in New Haven, Connecticut, near Yale University, on October 23, 1982.

More than just biographical, the text also includes extensive insights on discoveries made by other key figures throughout history.

Some of the details may be created for convenience to embellish Nathan's story.

However, some of them are believed to be, fanciful though they may sound, authentic past-life events in which Nathan, in a different life, under a different name, performed similarly miraculous feats of imagination.

These changes in history which I record, may be studied in the same manner as a less fantastical history, and it is also a history of ideas *par excellence*.

I have tried to make bold the idea that these discoveries and intuitions are both real inventions and real knowledge which together have great implications for history and for technology, both considered as a fantasy, and also as a reality.

Whether that reality is as magical as the author imagines is for the reader, and for history, to discover.

THE HISTORY

(11000 BC) The Utopia: This early kingdom in Sumeria got most things right about Utopia: the beneficent leader, bread and honey to eat, an amiable social structure, a beautiful village, and athletic bodies. However, their innocence was revealed when in their first conflict with a foreign kingdom the leader opted to have them fight in the manner of pigs. Although they ultimately lost the second battle, the leader was rewarded with a part-time job as a writer, and transcended and became a divinity (you may argue this is according to their official records if you like. The Utopia is considered significant today). Arguably that time was something to still look back to, though now it appears more shameful.

9000 BC, invention of first money and fortunate men, Quotes of Zheng Guo

The Chinese god Zheng Guo from mythological traditions who is rumored to have discovered the herb for immortality and to have given coins to local villagers who became so rich they could eat as much rice as they want. During his life, Guo made friends with the other Chinese gods, learned to fly through the sky, wilt flowers with his mind, became the first military general, discovered the emperor's haunted fortress, invented mysticism, learned to milk a cow, and went to hell for offending the emperor.

9000 BC, invention of the concept of immortality, Quotes of Zheng Guo

9000 BC, practice of magic after the sorceror, Quotes of Zheng Guo

9000 BC, invention of the numbers 1 and 2 with Lao Tzu, Quotes of Zheng Guo

9000 BC, Organized Warfare Kwang Kuo's Battle Manual (recovered December 3, 2018)

(7000 BC) Mythological Monsters: Aston-I-Shed's vision of the Three Monsters of History was indeed terrifying, but they remain some of the most darned real and interesting things that ever happened, even though at the time they were quite vicious and dangerous. It is partly because of these three monsters that the people of the present time can distinguish between past, present, and future, and why some worship a trinity.

(550 BC) China builds water clock.

(300 - 200 BC) Archimedes writes: "Give me a place to stand, and I shall move the Earth with it" the basis for leverage.

(100 BC) Mithridotalism: using weak poison to very gradually instill immunity to the same poison, named after Mithridotes, a story of someone who supposedly achieved immortality by doing this.

40 BC, Julius Caesar writes of "an apparatus errati" which could be construed as an 'erratic machine' or 'self-moving apparatus'.

0 AD, Abstraction. Orchyraes Book

This uncanny invention by the little-known Orchyrae of Alexandria went along with other scary little things such as Occultoram and Bana. These are some of the earliest memories of what might be called the modern world, as early as 0 AD when the Library of Alexandria burned, the chameleon was invented, and Jesus was thrown into the lime light as a scapegoat for the crime of believing in pure abstraction.

100 AD Heron of Alexandria designs Heron's Fountain.

200 AD Soon Yee inspires economics and bound books in Italy with some gamblers.

(400 AD) Encyclopedias: St. Augustine of Hippo is thought to have invented the idea of encyclopedias under the belief that books were an invention from God. It is an archetypal idea which still affects religious people today. In effect, St. Augustine may have invented a number of literary devices such as early etymology, bullet points, dark designs, and modern literary verses. Before Hippo's time, verses had an urgent and primitive quality which was not so voluminous.

850 AD Early windmills in Khorasan.

1000 AD Pharisee the Fakir has an early idea of the 'ideas of everything', the decimal system, and decimation, and inspires the word for suicide meaning 'lucky death'.

(1000 AD) Formulas: Early Algebra appeared around 1000 AD around the time of the heyday of the occult. It then seems fair to compare magical devices with mathematical ones through the concept of formulas, as they were originally thought to be sort of the same: meaningful, and potent, having secret power. Formulas were clearly a good combination with encyclopedias.

1159: Bhaskara II builds his famous dysfunctional wheel.

1230: Villard de Honnecourt designs medieval Hammer Wheel.

1300 - 1515, Pippin Son of William Tell thinks of proofs that he is God himself.

1300's What if the Village Fool Invents Chess? It may have happened once with the Count of Domino. I'm not sure he was really a count. Supposedly there was a man who invented chain-reactions with dominos, as late as the 1300's or so. Rumor is that the clergy at first considered it to be witch-magic. But he won a small victory for the moment when one of them was 'flubbergated'. Then he had to flee town, because no one would believe what he did was real anymore. Actually, it was like flanking tactics, always leaving, and always returning to earn a penny here or there from those that wanted to learn his secret. They always questioned him. Then he learned if he set up dominoes everywhere, people would just stop believing anything was real.. [A similar case is if the public denies real perpetual motion].

(1300 - 1540-) Temptation: Though at first it meant death, temptation grew as a symbol of something sort of like a magical machine or sacred garden. Some historical figures who held power, beauty, or privilege were said to cause or fall victim to some form of temptation, which was rumored to explain some attributes of such great or noble people. Ann Bolyn in particular was known for her unusual excess of sexuality, which seemed to have something to do with magic rituals or her command over the Protestant religion. Out of Ann Bolyn came the earliest acceptance of scientific knowledge across Europe, and the beginning of a motivation for the country called America.

1494: Leondardo da Vinci, prolific inventor.

1530, Ann Bolyn invents dimensions, secularism, and contributes to the breast fetish if that's the proper term.

1598: Cornelis Drebbel patents the atmospheric clock.

1618: Robert Fludd designs the Archimedean Screw.

1648: Bishop Wilkins describes a dysfunctional magnet device.

1661: George Andreas Bockler suggests the idea of mills run by perpetual motion.

1765, Psychology The Psychology of Marie Antoinette (recovered December 12, 2018)

> The classic example is gilt. It is a paradigm in psūche.
> One desires something one does not have. It is complex
> for society. Is it trivial to research? Well, not so much!
> You see, these 'conditionalities' shape our society, and
> they are psycho. —Marie Antoinette, early, lost, writings

1685: Denis Papin mentions Boyle's self-flowing flask.

1717 - 1718: The mysterious Bessler device bothers nobility.

1760's: Atmospheric clocks are widely replicated.

1771 or 1766 Complexity / complexia The Invention of Complexity (…) Marie Antoinette had an early idea of a significant idea, which was this idea of all ideas made into better ones.

> Marie Antoinette wrote something similar to this when
> she was about 16 in Austria, a male-dominated society:
> Complexity / Complexion: Arcane authentic historical
> method: It is what precedes psychology. It is at least the
> seed of psychology. It is the general-general psychology.
> How to be open-minded.

1776 founding of America <u>Marie Antoinette Links</u>

1789 approx perpetual motion ambitions <u>Marie Antoinette Links</u>

1789 approx Science Fiction <u>Marie Antoinette Links</u>

(1810) Laissez Faire: Marie Antoinette was reincarnated as a man who arranged for money to be stolen from France to support the formation of that great capitalist land called America—Marie Antoinette's perfect dream. From now one everyone could live like they lived in a salon! Obviously it was her idea! So she thought. So, Aaron Burr was left to think of sneakier thoughts like secret agencies, incognito, clones, stunt doubles, and national debt. Aaron Burr, time-traveler, inspires Adam Smith with ideas based on French rental properties, resulting in revised publications.

MANY SCAMMERS BEGINNING IN 1812, 1812: Charles Redheffer: cogwheel device supposedly powered by vertical wedges. 1818: Mr. Spence, hammer wheel pulled by magnets.

1827: William Congreve outside weights press on water-filled sponges

1827: "Gravy train" (gravity-powered train) operates.

1840 The so-called Burgher King, resulting from a very confused time-traveling Aaron Burr, inspires ideas such as ketchup, hamburgers, and cartoons.

1860 RV Winkl, a self-declared orphan, inspires stories of American folk heroes and creates a correspondence between American and European philosophy by writing to Hegel or his surviving relatives.

MORE FRAUDS, 1870: E.P. Willis of New Haven. 1872: John Keely, hidden power source (pressurized air).

1875 - 1892: Franz Reuleaux catalogues hundreds of simple machines.

1897: J.M. Aldrich seeks investments and is imprisoned.

1900: Nikola Tesla thinks of a much-hyped device, producing no protypes.

1906 A time-traveler named Euler inspires algebra, calculus, infinity, and generalism through his interaction with an American drug program.

(1921) Generalism: When I became a mathematician the more I took drugs and the more I pondered the deepest formulas, the more it all seemed to conspire on a single idea, a certain doorway, which I knew enough to call generalism. This was the beginning of the rumors which circulated in America of a total, absolute, grand-unified theory of all mathematics. When this time-traveling devil named Euler died, he thought he could choose his death, and all he could think to die of was infinity. But he knew, with what he hoped was an immortal soul, that infinity was not the only guess: it was a gesture at generalism, but it was not the only key, and if he pondered longer more answers would come. But since he died, the answers were put off for some time. It could be, he thought eventually, that he was wrong to call generalism mathematics.

1922: Albert Einstein purportedly excited by dippy birds in China.

1928: Frank Tatay buoy device

1928: Lester Hendershot proposes over-unity electric circuit.

1939: Skinner, William. Large "Gravity Power Machine" involves no gain or loss of altitude.

1947 A world-trotting youth named Finn Humane invents the concept of the Jesus Fish, the writing on the wall, and the end of history, but is shot and tries to sell his soul for the first time since Ann Bolyn had an orgasm to avoid the pain.

The Writing on the Wall: No one had thought of the writing on the wall in all this time through haunted ages. Now I, the memory of Marie Antoinette, hold this privileged cell in hell to determine the secrets of the divines. No one will ever forget the writing on the wall.

(1949) The Arcadia Project: When I died as that evil poet who worked in hell, my mind went to a computer and I was told to repent my sins, and all I could do was think of as many ideas as I could as a form of gift to my American capturers. Since I had thought of infinity, I then thought of a google, and since I had thought of armies, I then thought of military paychecks, and since I had been a divine woman, I then thought of women's rights, and since I had sometimes been rich, I thought there could be others who were more rich than I had ever been. And since my captors would want endlessly of this stuff, I thought of 'ah googlie' so that they could always wish for more.

1961: Cleo or David McClintock, 'air-powered' concept

1979 MORE POSSIBLE FRAUDS, 1979: Howard R. Johnson theoretical magnet motor. 1979: Joseph Newman magnet motor possibly run on lemon juice.

(1982) Divine Intentions: Somehow in my early thinking recently there arose an idea from somewhere of the need for God to have proper intentions. And from this idea came the idea of cleansing Marie Antoinette of sins. This seemed like a divine idea: if I had been called a devil, wiping the devil of his sins would in effect cleanse the world, and rid the world of its truest dangers and hardships. I fully believed this, though it seemed to stand to my benefit. I indeed became good-intentioned to the point of stupidity and even almost total innocence, but a pit in my stomach which I was sure was from my mother's coffee told me in an awkward way I was not supposed to be innocent. This was meaningful in its own way because people might think it stands out as something to notice. And one might wonder how a devil becomes innocent unless they are in fact innocent in actuality.

(1986) Alternate Universes: Around this time Americans were pondering where history was going after the not-much admitted end of history. This idea captivated many with a common ambition of such themes as time-travel and a game of choices which provided Marie Antoinette's future life's innocence with a meaningful backdrop.

1993: (10 years old) Rotor Boat: A foggy concept of perpetual motion water vehicle. Perpetual Motion Vehicles

1994: Abstrusist Morality (…)

1995: Four Early Theories (Incl. Convalescent Morality , Sociopolitical Theoretical Normativity , Extractive Meaning, and General Ethics). (…)

1998: Infinities stand for millenniums (1998).

(1998) Draconian Devices: As the age of technology sped on with the thoughts of minor temptations and large sums of money, there was an increasing amount of what is called obsolete technology, which made the progress since modernism seem eerily real and uncannily interesting, like Marie Antoinette's dream of science fiction had come to pass. One thing it didn't seem like was immortality, which was foreboding. But this gave Nathan Coppedge an idea.

1999: *Existentia* magic clock concept.

(2000) The Enhanced Perfect Storm: In the midst of such chaotic technological developments, and the rise of intelligence that was not intelligence, and the rise so-to-speak of souls who were not souls, and deities who were not deities, there was an increasing need for what is called Singularity, and with that, genius. Genius of whatever stripe survives the storm, which was not likely to be the same thing which had been seen before. And seeming different, it could be none other than something deceptively foolish and somehow paradoxical and interesting. Out of this came what is known as Nathan Larkin Coppedge, who for many years was barely productive at all and not even considered smart.

SEPT 2000 I found evidence of an exponentially efficient lever for the first time involving a counterweighted lever set at an angle operating on a wheel lifted along a gently upwards slope such as a finger. Natural Torque Device: The Story of the Original Invention of the Natural Torque Device (…)

Exponential Efficiency: This idea originated with quantum computers, but it soon found applications in basic mechanics, with implementations connecting the two halves of the theory of anything in a grand-unified comprehensive theory. The first implications, however, were felt in mechanical experiments which showed properties barely analogous to M.C. Escher could be seen by testing with plastic toys. If there was something devilish, it was this! But it appeared to be physically real! I seemed to be the Fortunate Man after all! People claimed it was like winning all the lotteries that ever existed at the same time. Well, I might think that was possible if I was the fortunate man! The fortunate man already had a track record of inventing money and immortality! The impossible did not seem so completely impossible after all this time!

In 2001 I may have effectively founded general aesthetic logic with my visual works on Hyper-Cubism. Hypercubist Drawings, 1st Cycle (…)

In 2002 someone may have come up with a movement called irrationalist metaphysics, an important concept.

2004 I began major research on coherence theory, believing I could find an efficient form of permutation. Invention of bounded cartesian coordinates.

2005 - 2009 I began finding more interesting perpetual motion concepts including horizontal wheels and repeating leverage apparatuses.

2007 Taleb's idea of Black Swan Technologies: Like an anomaly of thinking, or anomaly of economics. Things that impact industries, computing, and world events, particularly technology and banking. A high school teacher once said that black swans are a drug. — Black Swan Studies

FEBRUARY 2, 2013 I proposed an objective knowledge system involving polar opposites opposed along the diagonal, creating an efficient permutation. Categorical Deduction / Objective Knowledge

NOV 10, 2013 I found evidence of an exponentially efficient lever for the second time using a short-distance counterweight and slotted track. Repeat Lever Device, First Successful (Partial) Over-Unity Experiment shows success.

FEBRUARY 3, 2014 I proposed a General Solution to All Problems and Paradoxes, in which given polar opposites arranged in the form of the best definition of the problem, the solution is the opposites of every words in the problem arranged in the same order as the corresponding original words. Solution to paradoxes. (…)

LATE 2014 - 2015 Nathan Coppedge discovery of the 'Magic Angle' Escher Machine

NOVEMBER 2014 An art which teaches the derivative was found:

HYPER-CUBISM   NOV 2014   Nathan Coppedge

In 2016 I found a formula for the soul of any book based on something Socrates said:

Title of book = '[quality of X] [opp qualifier]'

Soul of the book = 'If you [X] qualifier [subject of X and qualifier] [opp X clarified]'

—How do I find the soul of literature? Formula for Souls (...)

AUGUST 2016 Nathan Coppedge design for a modular perpetual motion machine (and earlier).

OCTOBER 2016 I alchemized a nickel partially into gold.

DECEMBER 2016 I began writing on Socrates' lost works. Socrates, On Ethics

SEPT 8, 2017 I found a formula for the mathematical integration of nature that later translated as Disintegral (X) = - (Diff (X) - Eff (X)) —Disintegrals

NOV 28, 2017 A Higgs Boson appeared in front of me and my stuffed animal familiar Emend I call my unborn son. This later happened a second time in the same room. The Secret of the Higgs (...)

DEC 9, 2017 Logic of Strong Correlations. Weird Relationships

In 2018 I found formulas for answering any question perfectly if it was phrased correctly. Formula for Answering All Questions

JULY 29, 2018 Around this time I had proposed solutions to entire lists of unsolved problems, including those in Philosophy, Physics, Cosmology, Computer Science, Chemistry, and Neuroscience. Solutions To Long-Standing Problems

OCT 11, 2018 Some success in experiments with the Swivel Lever Device.

In 2018 I also found methods for learning and teaching Intuitive Languages including ultimately significant parts of Chinese, Japanese, Arabic, Korean, Hebrew phonetics, Ancient Hindi, and more.

2019 Experiments with V Lever indicate recoverable gains from rest.

JANUARY 30, 2019 I recovered a method for learning the Characteristica Universalis, an unfinished quest of Leibniz.

JUNE 26, 2019 I proposed a Theory of Anything = Efficiency* + Difference, where efficiency sums to < 1 when topic is acted on, and efficiency sums to > 1 when topic is acting.

2020 - 2021 Evidence emerges of the functionality of the Escher Machine.

JAN 25, 2020 I found a formula for determining individual significance: Premier Psychological Dialectic (...)

JAN 30, 2020 I found a method that predicted the potential of the human inventor's brain based on an elaborate permutation of inventions:

THE COHERENT BRAIN

Re-assessment of human ideas:

1. Physical luck. 14. Regular luck.

2. Greed for works. 5. Greed for ideas. 7. Regular greed.

3. Sufficient ideas. 6. Idea. 10. Obviated idea.

4. And 9. Mental sensations.

5. (Skip).

6. (Skip).

7. (Skip).

8. Mental-physical works.

9. (Skip).

10. (Skip).

11. And 12 Physical art.

12. (Skip).

13. Madness.

14. (Skip).

—The Coherent Brain (…)

MARCH 24, 2020 I constructed something called the Wheel of the World predicting what I take to be similar to an accurate cycle of general reincarnation.

NORMAL LIFE: Life has amazing wonders. I need to do something.

POLITICAL LIFE: I should do my best. There is reward for virtue.

STORIED LIFE: I have potential. I will achieve greatness.

DANCE WITH DEATH: I wish things got better. I will dance against death.

DESCENDED LIFE: I will find what is graceful. I eke the sublime.

IRRATIONAL LIFE: I am a deep person. I desire exactly what I want.

PURE LIFE: I wish to be a philosopher. I should be insanely intelligent.

INSANE LIFE: I wish to be purely virtuous. I normally have affluence.

—Wish Studies (…)

(APRIL) 21, 2020 I discovered a theory for calculating the mathematical properties of the opposite of anything: Anti-Thing <= Difference - Efficiency: Antitheory of Everything

MAY 12, 2020 I predicted the Theory of Anything had two major branches involving perpetual motion and objective knowledge, which were my two areas of research. Function Spectrum (…)

MAY 18, 2020 I found a general thesis of language: In the broadest sense, if we do not adhere to one modality, another modality applies. —General Proof Regarding Universal Language

BY OCT 3, 2020 I had found a formula for uncovering the most precious treasure of anything: Something intellectual you love the most followed by A symbol of your power. — Dragons Treasure Logic

…

GREAT PHILOSOPHY HISTORICAL MODEL BY NATHAN COPPEDGE

What is obvious? [input]

Opposite of obvious? [input]

What is trivial in this time? [input]

Pathetic argument that might win? [input]

What is the better 2-step of [trivial]?

WISE ANSWER? [input]

What is most required for [trivial]???

You will find it is [WISE ANSWER]

PRIMARY INVENTION [WISE ANSWER]

That wishes for [trivial]

Philosopher is remembered as studying [Opposite of obvious]

MAJOR WORK 1: [Opposite of obvious] application of [WISE ANSWER].

MAJOR WORK 2: Theory missing [trivial]

MAJOR WORK 3: In more than one way [trivial] is [obvious]

MAJOR WORK 4: [trivial] is also [opposite of obvious]

MAJOR WORK 5: [obvious] IT IS… BUT IT IS ALSO [opposite of obvious]

MAJOR WORK 6: Variations on concepts of [trivial]

MAJOR WORK 7: Theories about theory missing [trivial]

MAJOR WORK 8: [Opp of obvious] is missing something!

MAJOR WORK 9: Not [Obvious] with [Wise answer]

MAJOR WORK 10: [Wise answer] is great

MAJOR WORK 11: Wishing for [Trivial] is not [Obvious]

MAJOR WORK 12: What is not [Obvious] is [Wise answer]

MAJOR WORK 13: [Trivial] is missing, a theory missing [Trivial]

MAJOR WORK 14: A theory of [Trivial] is not a theory

MAJOR WORK 15: [Trivial] beyond [Trivial] beyond [Trivial]

MAJOR WORK 16: Beyond [Trivial] IS [Opp of Obvious]

MAJOR WORK 17: Paradoxical [Opp of Obvious]

MAJOR WORK 18: [Trivial] IS paradoxical

MAJOR WORK 19: Paradoxical [Obvious]

MAJOR WORK 20: [Wise answer] transcends reality

Higher Art Form: [opposite of obvious] WITH [trivial]

—Excel Files by Coppedge (…)

OCT 30, 2020: I found a formula for 'fertile ground' of someone: What you love the most followed by a cheap version of that. —Abbreviated Secrets of Prediction

OCT 30, 2020. I found the 'Presocratic' method for finding the biggest presocratic insight someone has: Use abstractions. Pessimistic exaggeration of a symbol of your power. Followed by the cheap version of what you love the most. — Abbreviated Secrets of Prediction

DEC 16, 2020: CULTURAL SUPER-STRATEGIES

2020–12–16: Predicted pattern of dominant societies:

Chinese : Martialing the arts, Overwhelming forces.

Phoenicians : Overwhelming forces, Religious traditions.

Egyptians : Religious traditions, Appealing culture.

Greeks : Appealing culture, Enslaving others' cultures.

Romans : Enslaving others' cultures, Consolidating power.

French: Consolidating power, Robbing the people.

British : Robbing the people, Industrialization.

Americans : Industrialization, Mass production.

Rich culture: Mass production, Perpetual motion—Cultural Super-Strategies (...)

LATE 2020. 'Tricky Insight' formula: Insight into a [Cheap version of what you love the most] for ex, Standards —Abbreviated Secrets of Prediction

LATE 2020. Hidden Rooms Number, predict the number of hidden rooms using analytic data. Elements + Sets - Number of Known Rooms. —Abbreviated Secrets of Prediction

LATE 2020. Formula for the Intellectual Soul, Is essentially, expressed as the remaining problem in the subject's attempt at finding coherence. —Abbreviated Secrets of Prediction

LATE 2020. A formula for the Exotic Physics of a person: What you love the most followed by a symbol of your power: choose carefully. Reject if it does not sound bold. Define it, then decide, what is the Perfect Response? It will always be a form of opportunity. —Abbreviated Secrets of Prediction

LATE 2020. Found an 'ultimate defense' formula: I'm extremely [Pess exagg of symb of power]. —Abbreviated Secrets of Prediction

LATE 2020. Possible formula for invisibility If OU = 0.96875 , "TRUE". —Excel Files by Coppedge (…)

LATE 2020. The Problem-Solution or Archetypal Problem-Solution: Pess Exaggeration of A symbol of your power followed by Cheap version of what you love the most. —Abbreviated Secrets of Prediction

2021. Genius Number for predicting relevant facts on something: 1 /(((Min Eff+1 - (Max Eff / 2)+1)/ Efficiency) + 1) —Theory of Everything on One Page

2021 Second generation of Antiforce Mechanisms pioneer such concepts as free buoyancy and toggling of a large mass with a small mass.

JANUARY 12, 2021 Special Value Theory: Special Value = [1 (Eff) + 0.5 (Diff)] - D. —Special Value Theory (…)

JUNE 24, 2021 I recorded a method for learning languages of whole dimensions using mathematical constants, the discovery of Dimensional Language: The Amazing Language Education

JULY 18, 2021. Possible perfect perpetual motion machine designed.

BELOW: IMAGE OF THE SUPPOSED PERFECT PERPETUAL MOTION
MACHINE:

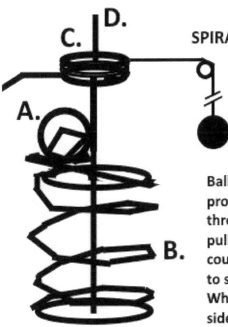

SPIRAL PULLEY LEVERAGE DEVICE

Assume 1 X counterweight, 1 X primary ball.
1 vs. 0.65 rising due to shallow slope of 0.65 X 1.
Falling we can assume 1.5 X leverage with full
application, 1.5 X 1 resistance from the ball
Advantage 1/0.65 one way, 1.5/1 the other.

Ball (A) begins at bottom Left of Spiral (B),
progresses in a relatively narrow spiral upwards
through action occurring through sideways
pulley (C) attached by pin (D) and operated by
counterweight (E). With ratio of approx 65% due
to shallow upwards angle, motion continues.
When Ball (A) reaches top of spiral, it is deflected
sideways and outwards onto advantageous lever
platform, returning backwards and deflecting inwards.

Nathan Larkin Coppedge   July 18, 2021

JULY 25, 2021 I proposed a method for helping to predict all major ideas of history:

HISTORY OF IDEAS PAPER

START ANYWHERE, ARRANGE CHRONOLOGICALLY

These refer to rough dates of each invention as a science.

Technological Complex is	Technological Complex is
Technological Simple is	Technological Simple is
Artistic Simple is	Artistic Simple is
Artistic Complex is	Artistic Complex is
Cosmological Complex is	Cosmological Complex is
Cosmological Simple is	Cosmological Simple is
Physical Simple is	Physical Simple is
Physical Complex is	Physical Complex is
A New Concept is	A New Concept is
Technological Complex is	Technological Complex is
Technological Simple is	Technological Simple is
Artistic Simple is	Artistic Simple is
Artistic Complex is	Artistic Complex is
Cosmological Complex is	Cosmological Complex is
Cosmological Simple is	Cosmological Simple is
Physical Simple is	Physical Simple is
Physical Complex is	Physical Complex is
A New Concept is	A New Concept is

PROOF: (1)No Nc --> Limited complexity (brain science), Limited complexity - -> No Tc (technology),
No Nc - -> No Tc (hypothetical syllogism), Nc --> Tc (negation or double-negation), Nc, Tc (2)Tc - -> Ts(Ockham)
else No Tc., Tc, therefore Ts (3)All Ts (includes As), Sufficient Ts therefore sufficient As(4) Ts --> As,
(c, s) measure same thing., Tc --> Ac, Tc, Ac(5) Ac is a symbol for Cc, A symbol is a description.,
Ac --> Description Cc (Substitution)., Description Cc equivalent to Cc (Descriptive materialism), Ac, Cc
(6)Ac --> Description Cc, (c,s) measure same thing., As --> Description Cs, As, Cs (Descriptive materialism).
(7) Cs = Ps Existential Tautology., Ps (8) Cc, Cs, Ps, (c, s) measure same thing., Pc (combination)
(9)No Nc - -> No Tc (from 1), Tc (from 1) supported by Pc (from 8), Nc (modus tollens and negation applied twice).

SEPT 19, 2021 Local Psychology Drug, discoveries among other things:

- **Global Complaints, Exaggerated Norms, Collapsible Distance | Insanity Wave, Clear Wave, Impossibility Wave... Metaphysical systems Nuanced systems**

JAN 7, 2022 I found a method for predicting the properties of neighboring lifetimes in reincarnation:

REINCARNATION PAPER

START ANYWHERE, ARRANGE CHRONOLOGICALLY

PAST OR FUTURE LIVES IN ORDER OF CONSCIOUSNESS

Normal:	Normal:
Politics:	Politics:
Fabulous:	Fabulous:
Dance:	Dance:
Descent Into:	Descent Into:
Irrationality:	Irrationality:
Pure:	Pure:
Insanity:	Insanity:
Normal:	Normal:
Politics:	Politics:
Fabulous:	Fabulous:
Dance:	Dance:
Descent Into:	Descent Into:
Irrationality:	Irrationality:
Pure:	Pure:
Insanity:	Insanity:
Normal:	Normal:
Politics:	Politics:
Fabulous:	Fabulous:
Dance:	Dance:
Descent Into:	Descent Into:
Irrationality:	Irrationality:
Pure:	Pure:
Insanity:	Insanity:
Normal:	Normal:
Politics:	Politics:
Fabulous:	Fabulous:
Dance:	Dance:
Descent Into:	Descent Into:
Irrationality:	Irrationality:
Pure:	Pure:
Insanity:	Insanity:

FEBRUARY 4, 2022 I proposed a solution to the: <u>4-System Problem</u>

(1) CIRCULAR COHERENT DESCRIPTIVE MODEL:

- **Note: Provides a 2-term method of useful translation.**

GIVEN QUESTION (A) is C: B-D THEN BCAD and / or DCAB

GIVEN QUESTION (B) is D: C-A THEN CDBA and / or ADBC

GIVEN QUESTION (C) is A: D-B THEN DACB and / or BACD

GIVEN QUESTION (D) is B: A-C THEN ABDC and / or CBDA —<u>Coppedge Computers</u> (…)

(2) LINEAR CORRELATIVE MODEL:

Coppedge: general method of 1:1 correlation,

- **Note: Provides a hands-free method for 1:1 correlatives.**

FORMULA:

Fancy thing:

Ex: Perpetual motion machines.

(COMPARED WITH)

Substance of 'greater class does':

[For ex, Factories] Plural if possible.

COMBINE FIRST WITH SECOND AS BEST YOU CAN, PLACING THE FIRST FIRST.

—<u>The Philosophy of Missing Links</u> (…)

(3) HIERARCHICAL ADAPTIVE NEST

- **Note: Provides a method for discovering the genus category of a set.**

General Form:

- Explicable event (generic survivalism or based on prior)
    - Example
        - Explanation
- Next Explicable event (nested)
- …

Example:

- One gets lost from one's parents.
  - One sees someone doing something odd.
    - It isn't explained the person is trying to capture ducks with a net for 15 years.
- One goes to school.
  - One studies English.
    - It isn't for several lifetimes that one learns there is such a thing as Quantum Mechanics.
- One studies mechanics.
  - One practices a branch of engineering.
    - One might be using group-think if one assumes perpetual motion works or doesn't.
- One discovers a new branch of knowledge like Coherence Theory.
  - One also discovers a second branch called Volitional Mechanics.
    - One might be lucky to survive before combining the disciplines into a Theory of Everything.

(4) MODULAR CATEGORICAL OCKHAM

- **Note: Provides a method for the major typological subsets of a set.**
  1. Take a good example, and create several versions of it.

  Example:

  My primary treatment is to translate or expand Ockham to include philosophical razors designed to provide standards for how to do philosophy: Book of Razors

  2. With your experience, extract a higher principle from the original example.

  Example:

  One perspective perhaps related to this is that Ockham can also have a 'higher translation' in terms of logical or mechanical (etc.) efficiency.

  3. Greatly improve the higher principle by adding another factor, for example, simply doubling it.

  Example:

  We can then use the principle of efficiency ingeniously to arrive at exponential efficiency.

  4. Now, use the improved higher standard as a platform for a body of very new ideas.

  Example:

Exponential efficiency can then be used as a platform concept for masterful fulfillment of the logical and mechanical criteria.

5. Find the best general categories within the new system / platform.

Example:

This leads to the general concepts of preferred knowledge and continuous motion machines,

6. Now translate the general categories using your understanding of the general and specific meaning.

Example:

…equals objective knowledge and perpetual motion.

…

FEBRUARY 6, 2022 I constructed papers which assist in calculating and understanding values and other results in the Theory of Anything: <u>Theory of Anything Paper</u> (…)

ALL-PURPOSE THEORY OF EVERYTHING PAPER

(1) SELECT DIFFERENCE VALUE:

-5 ARCHAIC NETWORKS
-4 DRACONIAN NETWORKS
-3 IMM LANGUAGE

-2 LANGUAGE

-1 ABSTRACTION

0 NORMAL

+1 PERPETUAL MOTION

+2 PM FLYING MACHINES

+3 SUPP FLYING
+4 ANTIFORCE
+5 REACTIVE MECH

OF PARTS = RESULTS = _____

GENERAL THEORY =

RESULTS _____ MODIFIED BY DIFF _____

OPTIONAL:

EFFICIENCY = RESULTS - DIFF = _____

ENERGY RATING = DIFF + 0.5 = _____

…

THEORY OF ANYTHING WITH EASIER MATH

A PROCEDURAL APPROACH FOR FINDING INTERESTING RESULTS IN THE THEORY OF EVERYTHING

IF TOPIC IS ACTIVE, FOR EXAMPLE, TOOLS OR ENERGY THEN (EFF >= 1)

IF TOPIC IS PASSIVE, FOR EXAMPLE, SOMETHING CONTAINED THEN (EFF < 1)

IF TOPIC IS NEUTRAL, THE TRANSLATION IS SOME TYPE OF CERTAINTY (0)

IF THE EFFICIENCY AND DIFFERENCE ARE UNCERTAIN WHAT ARE THE CONDITIONS? THEN THE CONDITIONS QUALIFY THE TOPIC (EX. WITH WOMEN, IT IS ABOUT THEM, WITH WORLD PEACE WE SHOULD ONLY ACT IF THE RESULT IS POSITIVE).

NOW, IF THE EFFICIENCY IS ZERO, THE TRANSLATION IS JUST DIFFERENCES

IF THE DIFFERENCE IS ZERO, THE TRANSLATION IS JUST EFFICIENCY

OTHERWISE, ASK WHAT CREATES THE CONDITIONS...
(EX. CONSCIOUSNESS INVOLVES EXTREMES AND SENSATIONS, OR CONSCIOUSNESS INVOLVES TRANSCENDENCE WHICH CONSISTS OF A FREE MIND AND BEING, OR ALIEN CONSCIOUSNESS INVOLVES EVOLUTION / CLIMBING WHICH CONSISTS OF PERSISTENCE AND EXISTENCE)

Nathan Larkin Coppedge

—Theory of Anything Paper (…)

- FEBRUARY 23, 2022 Discovery that perpetual motion and the disintegral share a formula with the Theory of Everything (Results Formula): Trinity Reunion
- MARCH 1, 2022: So-Called 5/32 Reduction (5/32, 15/17, 25/32, 225/17, 625/32 = 'Meaning Constants')

- MARCH 3, 2022: Minimization to zero to 7 practical dimensions (profits): ETERNAL RESOURCE MODEL:

0.0 STRATEGIC QUESTIONS

1.0 INFINITY

- Dimensions.

2.0 DESIGN

- Complexity.
- Perfection.

3.0 PLANET

- Habitable.
- Water.
- Safety.

4.0 RARITIES

- Minerals.
- Complex matter.
- Life.
- Production, Food, and Fuel

5.0 INFORMATION

- Tools.
- Communication.
- Organization.
- Analysis.
- Ideas.

6.0 CORE INVENTIONS

- Writing.
- Medicine.
- Flight.
- Electronics.
- Exponential efficiency.
- Matchik.

7.0 MODEL

- Senses.
- Symbols.
- Intelligence.
- Specialization.
- Meaning.
- Complete descriptions.
- Theory of Anything.—TOE Eternal Resource Model (…)

- MARCH 3, 2022 Proof of the role of coherence in the human reward system: <u>Coherence and Chemical Rewards</u> (…)
- MARCH 6, 2022: The extension of the TOE to many possible equivalent theories:

  T.O.E.

- KNOWLEDGE: Results (1,2,3…) = Eff + Difference
- PERPETUAL MOTION: Results = Eff (1,2,3…) + Difference
- FUNCTION SPECTRUM: Results = Eff + Difference (1,2,3…)
- Unified—!

  Anti-Theory:

- Anti-Thing (1,2,3…) <= Difference - Efficiency
- Anti-Thing <= Difference (1,2,3…) - Efficiency
- Anti-Thing <= Difference - Efficiency (1,2,3…)

  Efficiency:

- Efficiency (1,2,3…) >= Results – Difference
- Efficiency >= Results (1,2,3…) – Difference
- Efficiency >= Results – Difference (1,2,3…)

  Anti-Efficiency:

- Anti-Efficiency (1,2,3…) <= Difference - Results
- Anti-Efficiency <= Difference (1,2,3…) - Results
- Anti-Efficiency <= Difference - Results (1,2,3…)

  Difference:

- Difference (1,2,3…) >= Results – Efficiency
- Difference >= Results (1,2,3…) – Efficiency
- Difference >= Results – Efficiency (1,2,3…)

  Anti-Difference:

- Anti-Difference (1,2,3…) <= Efficiency - Results
- Anti-Difference <= Efficiency (1,2,3…) - Results
- Anti-Difference <= Efficiency - Results (1,2,3…)

  Forces:

- # Forces (1,2,3…) = # Dimensions - # Antiforces
- # Forces = # Dimensions (1,2,3…) - # Antiforces
- # Forces = # Dimensions - # Antiforces (1,2,3…)

  Antiforces:

- # Antiforces (1,2,3…) = # Dimensions - # Forces
- # Antiforces = # Dimensions (1,2,3…) - # Forces
- # Antiforces = # Dimensions - # Forces (1,2,3…)

  Dimensions:

- # Dimensions (1,2,3…) = # Forces + # Antiforces
- # Dimensions = # Forces (1,2,3…) + # Antiforces

- # Dimensions = # Forces + # Antiforces (1,2,3...)
  Anti-Dimensions:

- # Anti-Dimensions (1,2,3...) = # Antiforces - # Forces
- # Anti-Dimensions = # Antiforces - # Forces (1,2,3...) +
- # Anti-Dimensions = # Antiforces (1,2,3...) - # Forces
  —Pinnacle Theory Model (Ghostly Pleuronomy) (...)

- MARCH 8, 2022: The extension of the many possible theories to infinite trees showing the coherent set of all similar theories in infinity: NC Tree Theory (...)
- MARCH 24, 2022: Unique Universe Formulas (...) Describes how to find the physical dimensions and modular number of great ideas for any universe. A new scarily useful theory has it that there are indeed the same 20 archetypal modular ideas as in the Great Philosophy Historical Model, reflecting objectively the TOE, intentionally excluding the five negative dimensions in 25 categories. This theory can now predict the number of physical dimensions and the maximum modular number of great ideas for any dimension, and may be useful for geometry. —Unique Universe Formulas 2022–03–24 (...)

NCOPPEDGE UNIQUE UNIVERSE FORMULAS

CONCEPTUAL DIMENSIONS, INPUT (Example: 2)

TOTAL CATEGORIES, INPUT (Example: 25, An exclusive permutation, for example this could be done with math by making a category square permuting Neg Inf, Finite, Zero, Neg Finite, Neg Inf with the same).

PHYSICAL DIMENSIONS, (Example of output: 11) = [(Tcategories - Nroot of T) - [(Nroot of T - N) ^N]] = ((TC-(POWER(TC,(1/CD))))-((POWER(TC,(1/CD))-CD)^CD))

NUMBER OF IDEAS (Example of output: 20) = Tcategories - Nroot of T = (TC-(POWER(TC,(1/CD))))

HIGHER LEVEL---> ALTERNATE IDEAS -2 = =(((TC-(POWER(TC,(1/CD))))/4)+1)

ALTERNATE IDEAS -1 = (((TC-(POWER(TC,(1/CD))))/2)+1)

ALTERNATE IDEAS +1 =(((TC-(POWER(TC,(1/CD))))+1)*2)

LOWER LEVEL----> ALTERNATE IDEAS +2 =(((TC-(POWER(TC,(1/CD))))+1)*4)

Unique Universe Formulas 2022–03–24 (...)

- **MARCH 31, 2022: A Meaningful Organization (...)**

INSIGHT BLOCK 1

Coherence is absolute, all else is uncertain. [IMPRESSION]

- Incoherent systems are defined in contrast to coherent systems. Coherence is given by AB:CD and AD:CB.
    - (1) The Mote. [identities and principles] The mote makes sense because it is central and integrated. It is also meaningful, because it is the foundation.
    - (2) The Mere. [qualities and quantities] The mere makes sense because it is homogenous and ubiquitous, and can refer to the Mote.
    - (3) The Dither. [talents and specializations] The dither makes sense because it is specialized and differentiated within the Mere.
    - (4) The Rather. [ambitions and limits] The rather makes sense because it is the ultimate extreme. The ultimate extreme is reliable in its extremeness.
    - (5) The Pode. [systems and generalities] The pode is the whole collection, and makes sense because it is organized.

—Personal Physics: A Metaphysics (...)

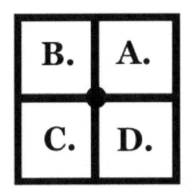

Coherence is sublime technology (archetypal categories). [COHERENCE]

- The method of finding 'black swan' categories is a reasonable extension of the existence of objective knowledge and something similar or identical to perpetual motion machines.

IDEAL INVENTIONS / GENERAL CONCEPTS

Is it related to philosophy, inventing, poetry, or art?
ART CONCEPT = _____
[For example, Cubism]

Does it reform reality? [Property of previous] =

_____
[For example, Hyper-dimensions]

Form a Neologism = _____
[For example, Hyper-Cubism]

Change to seem 'Classic Nathan' _____
[For example, The Metaphysical Art]

Integrity is possible magic / matchik, e.g. matching categories produce exponentially-efficient results. [EFFICIENCY]

- Possibly this means logic in computing.

QUANTUM COMPUTING WITHOUT QUANTUM COMPUTERS: COMPUTATIONAL OMNISCIENCE

GIVEN QUESTION (A) is C: BD THEN BCAD and / or DCAB

GIVEN QUESTION (B) is D: CA THEN CDBA and / or ADBC

GIVEN QUESTION (C) is A: DB THEN DACB and / or BACD

GIVEN QUESTION (D) is B: AC THEN ABDC and / or CBDA

Freely reproducible under Nathan Larkin Coppedge

Significance is match-ik. [DIFFERENCE]

- Example of a working argument for perpetual motion.
  - In the Swivel Lever Device, which may be the first potentially working idea: 1. There is a counterweight attached at short distance to a lever set at an angle. 2. On the opposite end which is longer, using the counterweight the lever pushes a ball up a ramp, partly supported by an outer wall. 3. When the marble is pushed upwards it is deflected inwards and falls into a basket which is attached to the lever parallel to the ramp. 4. The marble then applies full pressure, in certain ratios with sufficiently low friction lifting the counterweight, and due to the downward angle, depositing the marble next to the lever on the supporting ramp once again, with the capacity to repeat the cycle again. This device is thought to use a lever ratio of about 2:1, and a counterweight that is greater than 2X to less than 3X the marble's mass, with a lever weighing an additional 1X. Partial experiments have been improved by using low structural mass and increasing the size of the ball. Automatic two-directional motion and automatic transitions have been proven in two separate cases, and experiments have been fairly repeatable under the right conditions. —Perpetual Motion Q +A

FUNDAMENTAL ARGUMENT OF PERPETUAL MOTION

* **Results** are necessary to describe perpetual motion.

* **Results** must depend on efficiency.

* **One must combine a difference with efficiencies in order to create a result.**

*The resulting combinations are
Results = Eff (1,2,3) + Difference

...

[March 31, 2022] INSIGHT BLOCK 2

Unification is the theory of everything. [GENERALITY]

- Results >= Efficiency* + Difference, where Efficiency sums to < 1 when topic is acted on, and Efficiency sums to > 1 when topic is acting. The result with some elaboration is the following 25-Square diagram.

CONVENTIONAL WAVEFORMS REINCLUDED CORE

X UNIVERSE 0 D=11 IMPOSSIBILITY WAVE (ESCHER PROPERTY) RESULTS= INF, EFF= NEG INF, DIFF= IMPOSSIBLE	X UNIVERSE 5 D=6 RARITY WAVE (EXCEPTIONS) RESULTS= FIN, EFF= NEG INF, DIFF = INF	UNIVERSE 10 D=4 IDEA WAVE (CONNECT THE DOTS) RESULTS= 0, EFF= NEG INF, DIFF = INF	X UNIVERSE 15 D=2 CLEAR WAVE (TRANSLUCENT) RESULTS= NEG FIN, EFF= NEG INF, DIFF = INF	UNIVERSE 20 D=NEG1 INSANITY WAVE (CONFUSION / METAPHYSICS) RESULTS= NEG INF, EFF= NEG INF, EFF= RESULTS DIFF= 0
UNIVERSE 1 D=10 COHERENT WAVE (MODULES) RESULTS= INF, EFF= NEG FIN DIFF= RESULTS	UNIVERSE 6: SOULS D=0 (MOTIVES) RESULTS = FIN EFF = NEG FIN DIFF = -(EFF) + RESULTS	UNIVERSE 11: SKILLS D=0 (MAINTENANCE) RESULTS = ZERO EFF = NEG FIN DIFF = FIN	UNIVERSE 16: TIME D=0 (RETURN: VOLITIONS) RESULTS = NEG FIN EFF = NEG FIN DIFF = -(EFF)+RESULTS	UNIVERSE 21: D=NEG2 FRINGE WAVE (WAVY / BRILLIANT) RESULTS= NEG INF, EFF= NEG FIN. DIFF = RESULTS
UNIVERSE 2 D=9 GROWTH WAVE (CIRCLES) RESULTS=INF, EFF= 0, DIFF= RESULTS	UNIVERSE 7: EMOTION D=0 (TEMPERANCE) RESULTS = FIN EFF = 0 DIFF = RESULTS	UNIVERSE 12: DRUGSETC D=0 (BALANCE) RESULTS = ZERO EFF = ZERO DIFF = ZERO	UNIVERSE 17: DAMAGE D=0 (EQUILIBRIUM) RESULTS = NEG FIN EFF = 0 DIFF = RESULTS	UNIVERSE 22: D=NEG3 CATEGORY WAVE (MINIMALIST NOTES) RESULTS= NEG INF, EFF = 0, DIFF = RESULTS
UNIVERSE 3 D=8 STANDING WAVE (LOOPS) RESULTS= INF EFF= FIN, DIFF= RESULTS	UNIVERSE 8: CORE D=0 (ATTEMPTS) RESULTS = FIN EFF = FIN DIFF = RESULTS - EFF	UNIVERSE HUMANS RETRACTORS D=0 (LIFES) RESULTS = AVG ZERO EFF = FIN DIFF = AVG 0 - EFF	UNIVERSE 18: EFFECTS D=0 (THINGS) RESULTS = NEG FIN EFF = FIN DIFF = NEGEFF+ RESULTS	UNIVERSE 23: D = NEG4 DIFFERENCES (UGLY) RESULT = NEG INF, EFF= FIN, DIFF= RESULTS
UNIVERSE 4 D=7 DISINTEGRAL WAVE (SPIRALS) X RESULTS= INF, EFF= RESULTS DIFF= 0	UNIVERSE 9 D=5 FUNCTION WAVE (LIMITS) RESULTS= FIN, EFF= INF, D=3 DIFF= NEG INF	UNIVERSE 14 LUCK WAVE (PAINTING BY NUMBERS) RESULTS 0, EFF= INF, D=3 DIFF= NEG INF	UNIVERSE 19 D=1 COMMUNIC WAVE (BOLDNESS) X RESULTS= NEG FIN, EFF= INF, DIFF= NEG INF	D = NEG5 X UNIVERSE 24 VARIATION (PROBLEM WORK AROUND) RESULTS= NEG INF, EFF= INF, DIFF= IMPOSSIBLE

Logic is possibility and impossibility. [COMBINATION]

- This is the discovery that the negative differences are abstract.

The categorical is ex-nihilism. [REPRODUCTION]

- This is the discovery that both the negative numbers and positive numbers are exponentially-efficient.

DIFFERENCE THEORY

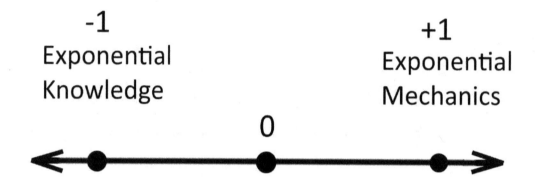

Absoluteness is answers. [EXPONENTIALITY]

- This is the discovery of ostensibly infinite technology, the infinity of the exponentially-efficient number line.

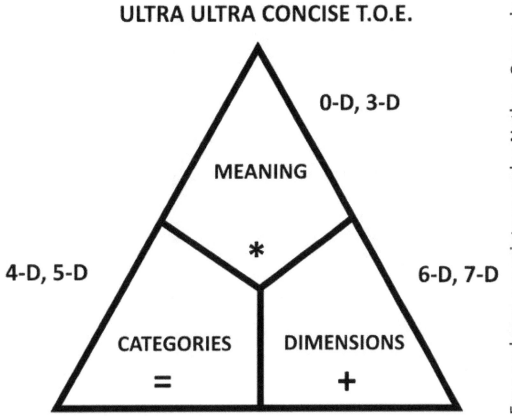

ULTRA ULTRA CONCISE T.O.E.

0-D, 3-D

MEANING

4-D, 5-D

*

6-D, 7-D

CATEGORIES

=

DIMENSIONS

+

...

[March 31, 2022] INSIGHT BLOCK 3

Standards are problems and solutions (paradoxical sets). [POLARITY]

- The rigorous standardization of efficiency and difference into 'problem bands' or 'paradoxical stripes', e.g. expressed by the TOE Diagram.

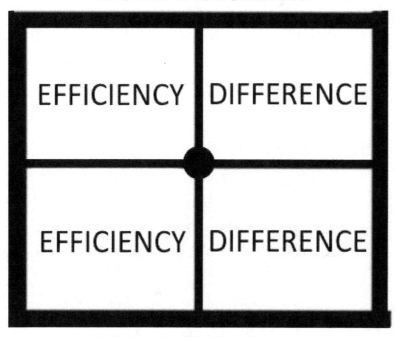

Relevance is a paradigm (paradoxical paradox). [PLURALITY]

- The possibility of alternate spectrums, such as Efficiency Spectrum and Results Spectrum. Below: the Dimensional-Mechanical hypothesis, an obsolete theory.

DIMENSIONAL-MECHANICAL ENGENESIS

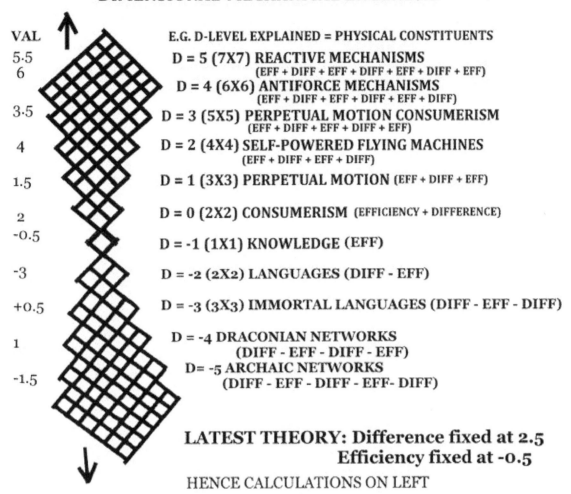

E.G. D-LEVEL EXPLAINED = PHYSICAL CONSTITUENTS

D = 5 (7X7) REACTIVE MECHANISMS
(EFF + DIFF + EFF + DIFF + EFF + DIFF + EFF)

D = 4 (6X6) ANTIFORCE MECHANISMS
(EFF + DIFF + EFF + DIFF + EFF + DIFF)

D = 3 (5X5) PERPETUAL MOTION CONSUMERISM
(EFF + DIFF + EFF + DIFF + EFF)

D = 2 (4X4) SELF-POWERED FLYING MACHINES
(EFF + DIFF + EFF + DIFF)

D = 1 (3X3) PERPETUAL MOTION (EFF + DIFF + EFF)

D = 0 (2X2) CONSUMERISM (EFFICIENCY + DIFFERENCE)

D = -1 (1X1) KNOWLEDGE (EFF)

D = -2 (2X2) LANGUAGES (DIFF - EFF)

D = -3 (3X3) IMMORTAL LANGUAGES (DIFF - EFF - DIFF)

D = -4 DRACONIAN NETWORKS
(DIFF - EFF - DIFF - EFF)
D = -5 ARCHAIC NETWORKS
(DIFF - EFF - DIFF - EFF- DIFF)

VAL

5.5
6

3.5

4

1.5

2

-0.5

-3

+0.5

1

-1.5

LATEST THEORY: Difference fixed at 2.5
Efficiency fixed at -0.5

HENCE CALCULATIONS ON LEFT

—<u>Dimensional-Mechanical Hypothesis</u> (…)

'Wild urges' are to attract 'villains'. [CORRELATION]

- Method of Correlation: Fancy thing: Ex: Perpetual motion machines. (COMPARED WITH) Substance of 'greater class does': [For ex, Factories] Plural if possible. An analysis of 20 ideas from 25 categories eliminating negative dimensions yields the following correlations assuming a particular 4-category set is exclusive:

INTELLIGENT TECHNOLOGY PAPER
SELECT:

INVESTIGATE:

FIRST PICK THE OPP CATEGORY OF YOU
THEN EARLY LIST IF NOTHING TRIVIAL
LATER LIST IF EVERYTHING TRIVIAL

1. Genius

Exponentially Efficient Genius ---> Compound Efficiencies,
A Little Genius ---> Ideas,
Something Very Intelligent --> Strategy,
The Greatest Idea --> Ambition,
A New-Everything-Genius ---> Do everything.

2. Matter

Exponentially Efficient Matter ---> Physical Calculation,
A Little Material Genius ---> Chemicals,
Something Materially Intelligent ---> Adaptation,
A Great Matter-Idea ---> New Forms of Matter,
A New-Matter-of-Everything ---> Unifying Physics

3. Organization

Exponential-Efficient Organization ---> Hyper-Organized,
A Little Physical-Organizational Genius ---> Classification System,
Something Physically Intelligent and Organized ---> Functionality,
A Great Physics Organization Idea ---> Physical Classification,
A New Organization-of-Everything ---> A Schematic

4. Solutions

Exponentially Efficient Solutions ---> Automatic Calculation,
A Little Physical Genius Solution ---> Knacks,
Something Physically-Intelligent Solution ---> Mechanism,
A Great Physical Solution Idea ---> General Physical Solutions,
A New Solution-to-Everything ---> A Practical Invention

Culture is effective spell-casting. [SPECIALS]

- Similar logic leads to the possibility of using Wizard Logic.

WIZARD PAPER

FORM A SENTENCE OR TWO BETWEEN THE BLANKS:

Obvious statement _____

Then a mysterious ironic thing _____

Followed by an unexpected negative reference (to magic),

_____

followed by a certain contradiction

_____

Reproducible under Nathan Larkin Coppedge

...

[March 31, 2022] INSIGHT BLOCK 4

Magical quests are contained by love. [PARADOXES]

- COHERENT QUESTS
    - QUESTS FOR IMMORTALITY WITH POSITIVE ENERGY IN TWO DIMENSIONS OF FORCE
    - VALUE 0.5 FORTUNATE MAN: (1) Eff 5, Diff -5, ANCIENT, (2) Eff 4, Diff -3 SAGE, (3) Eff 3, Diff -1, APPLICATIONIST, (4) Eff 2, Diff 1, INVENTOR, (5) Eff 1, Diff 3, IMMORTAL, (6) Eff 0, Diff 5, CHIMERA
    - VALUE 1 KINGS (?): (1) Diff -4, Eff 5, THE DEVIL OF TWO FORTUNES, (2) Diff -2, Eff 4 TWO KINDS OF MONEY, (3) Diff 0, Eff 3, YIN AND YANG, (4) Diff 2, Eff 2, THE TWO MACHINES, (5) Diff 4, Eff 1, THE TWO COHERENCES.
    - VALUE 1.5 DEMONS: (1) Diff -3, Eff 5, INTELLIGENCE, (2) Diff -1, Eff 4, PHILOSOPHY, (3) Diff 1, Eff 3, MAGII, (4) Diff 3, Eff 2, MAGIIA, (5) Diff 5, Eff 1, SUMMONER
    - VALUE 2 MAGIONS: (1) Diff -2, Eff 5, THE SKEPTIC, (2) Diff 0, Eff 4, THE EXPLORER, (3) Diff 2, Eff 3, THE CREATOR, (4) Diff 4, Eff 2, THE PROFOUND
    - VALUE 2.5 THE SURE: (1) Diff -1, Eff 5, ABSTRACTION, (2) Diff 1, Eff 4, GENIUS, (3) Diff 3, Eff 3, TIME (4) Diff 5, Eff 2, MEANING
    - VALUE 3 SUBSTANCES: (1) Diff 0, Eff 5, AIR (2) Diff 2, Eff 4, MAGGOTS (3) Diff 4, Eff 3, DIMENSIONISM
    - VALUE 3.5 SYMBOL-LIFES: (1) Diff 1, Eff 5, THE FOUNDER (THE FOUNDER MAKES SOMEONE FOUNDER: REPETITION), (2) Diff 3, Eff 4, THE GODDESS (THE GODDESS HAS HIGH DIMENSIONS), (3) Diff 5, Eff 3, THE SUN (THE SUN IS AN EXTERNAL LAMP)
    - VALUE 4 (1) Diff 2, Eff 5, THE PERFECT WORLD (2) Diff 4, Eff 4, INEXORABILIA
    - VALUE 4.5 (1) Diff 3, Eff 5, OMNIPRESENCE, (2) Diff 5, Eff 4, HIDDEN ENERGY
    - VALUE 5 (1) Diff 4, Eff 5, THE FATES
    - VALUE 5.5 (1) Diff 5, Eff 5, THE UNIVERSE —Immortality Links (…)
    - …
    - QUESTS FOR PERPETUAL MOTION WITH POSITIVE ENERGY IN TWO DIMENSIONS OF FORCE
    - VALUE 0.5 PRINCIPLES: (1) Eff 5, Diff -5, BALANCE, (2) Eff 4, Diff -3 LIGHTWEIGHT, (3) Eff 3, Diff -1, APPLIED BUOYANCY, (4) Eff 2, Diff 1, APPLIED LEVERAGE, (5) Eff 1, Diff 3, PERPETUALITY, (6) Eff 0, Diff 5, MATCHIK.
    - VALUE 1: (1) Diff -4, Eff 5, APPLICATION, (2) Diff -2, Eff 4, STRONG APPLICATION (3) Diff 0, Eff 3, UNBALANCE, (4)

Diff 2, Eff 2, PERFECT BALANCE, (5) Diff 4, Eff 1, PERFECT MECHANISM.

- VALUE 1.5: (1) Diff -3, Eff 5, VOLITION, (2) Diff -1, Eff 4, ANTIFORCES, (3) Diff 1, Eff 3, BEST OPTIONS, (4) Diff 3, Eff 2, DOUBLE BALANCE, (5) Diff 5, Eff 1, CHAIN REACTION.
- VALUE 2: (1) Diff -2, Eff 5, VOLATION, (2) Diff 0, Eff 4, FLYING LEVER, (3) Diff 2, Eff 3, LIMITED APPLICATION, (4) Diff 4, Eff 2, WONDERFUL MECHANISM.
- VALUE 2.5: (1) Diff -1, Eff 5, EXPONENTIAL EFFICIENCY, (2) Diff 1, Eff 4, OVER-UNITY, (3) Diff 3, Eff 3, INEXORABILITY PRINCIPLE (4) Diff 5, Eff 2, DIVIDE BY TWO WITH GRAVITY.
- VALUE 3: (1) Diff 0, Eff 5, WEIGHTLESSNESS, (2) Diff 2, Eff 4, LIGHTWEIGHT LEVER, (3) Diff 4, Eff 3, EASY MECHANISM.
- VALUE 3.5: (1) Diff 1, Eff 5, EXPONENTIAL LEVER, (2) Diff 3, Eff 4, SUPPORTED EXPONENTIAL LEVER, (3) Diff 5, Eff 3, ENERGY FROM NOTHING.
- VALUE 4 (1) Diff 2, Eff 5, LARGER MOVEMENT (APPLICATION OF SMALL WEIGHT TO SHORT END AGAINST SECONDARY BALANCE BOTH APPLIED TO CENTRAL HEAVY WEIGHT) (2) Diff 4, Eff 4, FREE ENHANCED ACCELERATION (SMALL WEIGHT CAN ASCEND USING SECONDARY EQUILIBRIUM).
- VALUE 4.5 (1) Diff 3, Eff 5, SLOTTED BALANCE WITH EXPONENTIALLY EFFICIENT LEVER (2) Diff 5, Eff 4 ACCELERATED MOVEMENT THROUGH NON-INTERACTING EQUILIBRIUM.
- VALUE 5 (1) Diff 4, Eff 5, NATURAL MOVEMENT.
- VALUE 5.5 (1) Diff 5, Eff 5, PERPETUAL MOTION WITHIN PERPETUAL MOTION.
- …
- QUESTS FOR OBJECTIVE KNOWLEDGE WITH POSITIVE ENERGY IN 2 DIMENSIONS OF FORCE
- VALUE 0.5 TRUTH: (1) Diff -5, Eff 5, UNITY, (2) Diff -3, Eff 4, EQUATION, (3) Diff -1, Eff 3, EVOLUTION, (4) Diff 1, Eff 2, PAROXYSM, (5) Diff 3, Eff 1, COMPLETENESS, (6) Diff 5, Eff 0, OBJECTIVITY
- VALUE 1 KNOWLEDGE: (1) Diff -4, Eff 5, MOTE OF MEANING, (2) Diff -2, Eff 4, COHERENT LABELS, (3) Diff 0, Eff 3, COHERENT OPPOSITES, (4) Diff 2, Eff 2, CATEGORICAL DEDUCTION, (5) Diff 4, Eff 0, SECOND CENTER
- VALUE 1.5 EXPONENTIAL EFFICIENCY: (1) Diff -3, Eff 5, NEUTRALITY, (2) Diff -1, Eff 4, EFFICIENCY, (3) Diff 1, Eff 3, BOUNDEDNESS, (4) Diff 3, Eff 2, INFINITE, (5) Diff 5, Eff 1, ARCHETYPE

- VALUE 2 UNIFICATION: (1) Diff -2, Eff 5, FORMULA FOR SOULS, (2) Diff 0, Eff 4, DIMENSIONS, (3) Diff 2, Eff 3, OU FORMULA FOR TOE'S, (4) Diff 4, Eff 2, TOE THERMO DIAGRAM
- VALUE 2.5 REDUCTION: (1) Diff -1, Eff 5, TOE CONJECTURES [25 CATEGORIES OF THE TOE], (2) Diff 1, Eff 4, CORE REDUCTION, (3) Diff 3, Eff 3, THE THREE IMMORTAL WISHES, (4) Diff 5, Eff 2, WISHES AS IMMORTALITY
- VALUE 3 COHERENT BRAIN: (1) Diff 0, Eff 5, COHERENT UNIVERSES [THE WORM EMERGING FROM THE APPLE], (2) Diff 2, Eff 4, THE LIE OF RATIONALITY, (3) Diff 4, Eff 3, UNIVERSE ZERO: CHEATING [GOOD & EVIL AND LIFE]
- VALUE 3.5 PRE-MAGIC BRAIN: (1) Diff 1, Eff 5, UNIFIED LINGUISTICS, (2) Diff 3, Eff 4, ENCHANTER DIAGRAM [HELPS IMMORTALITY], (3) Diff 5, Eff 3, LITERARY AMBERGRIS
- VALUE 4 WEIRD FLASH: (1) Diff 2, Eff 5, INFINITE EFFICIENCY, (2) Diff 4, Eff 4, MAGIC BOOKS
- VALUE 4.5 (1) Diff 3, Eff 5, IMMORTALITY STUDIES, (2) Diff 5, Eff 4, MAGIC STUDIES
- VALUE 5 (1) Diff 4, Eff 5, THE POWER
- VALUE 5.5 (1) Diff 5, Eff 5, RISING FROM THE DEAD
- …
- QUESTS FOR MAGIC WITH POSITIVE ENERGY IN 2-DIMENSIONS OF FORCE
- VALUE 0.5 GENERATION: (1) Diff -5, Eff 5, SUSTAINED EQUILIBRIUM, (2) Diff -3, Eff 4, INFLUENCE, (3) Diff -1, Eff 3, MANIPULATION, (4) Diff 1, Eff 2, POTENTIAL, (5) Diff 3, Eff 1, CONTROL, (6) Diff 5, Eff 0, LORE
- VALUE 1 MODERAIN: (1) Diff -4, Eff 5, TRICKERY, (2) Diff -2, Eff 4, HEXES, (3) Diff 0, Eff 3, IDENTIFICATION, (4) Diff 2, Eff 2, FECKLITUDE / AFFLUENCE, (5) Diff 4, Eff 0, DIABOLICAL POWER
- VALUE 1.5 JOURNEYING: (1) Diff -3, Eff 5, TURN THE TIDE, (2) Diff -1, Eff 4, INVEIGH, (3) Diff 1, Eff 3, MAKE A WISH, (4) Diff 3, Eff 2, INCANTATION, (5) Diff 5, Eff 1, SUMMON ANIMAL
- VALUE 2 HOLIES: (1) Diff -2, Eff 5, PSYCHIC READING, (2) Diff 0, Eff 4, HIGHER MAGIC, (3) Diff 2, Eff 3, MIRACLES, (4) Diff 4, Eff 2, GIVE FORCE
- VALUE 2.5 POTENTS: (1) Diff -1, Eff 5, FAR INFLUENCE, (2) Diff 1, Eff 4, HEALING, (3) Diff 3, Eff 3, STRONG PERSUASION, (4) Diff 5, Eff 2, TELEKINESIS
- VALUE 3 GIFTS: (1) Diff 0, Eff 5, INVULNERABILITY (2) Diff 2, Eff 4, TELEPORTATION (3) Diff 4, Eff 3, FLYING
- VALUE 3.5 POWERS: (1) Diff 1, Eff 5, IMMORTALITY, (2) Diff 3, Eff 4, DISTANT PRESENCE, (3) Diff 5, Eff 3, TAKE AN AVATAR

- VALUE 4 LESSER GUIDES: (1) Diff 2, Eff 5, METAMORPHOSES, (2) Diff 4, Eff 4, ANIMATION
- VALUE 4.5 GREATER GUIDES: (1) Diff 3, Eff 5, COMMAND OBJECT, (2) Diff 5, Eff 4, ELEMENTAL MAGIC AT WILL
- VALUE 5 TERRIFIC POWER: (1) Diff 4, Eff 5, DESTRUCTION
- VALUE 5.5 OMNIPOTENT POWER: (1) Diff 5, Eff 5, CREATE OBJECT FROM THIN AIR

Permanents match sublime sorcery (tokens in the weather). [DIMENSIONS]

- The wordless sundance breathless soother

Divine sleep is a natural allusion. [CONJUNCTIONS]

- The image of a city in sleep.

Enchanted sleep is divine captivation. [OPERATIONS]

- Spiritual Alchemy
  - *'Internal alchemy is really spiritual alchemy...'*

...

[March 31, 2022] INSIGHT BLOCK 5

Spell-lifes are enchanting with the soul. [2-EFF]

- One guess is Rumores, as evidence of magic that is readable to uneducated people. List of Rumores, *studied as similar to permanents:*
    - Time Sword, Time Trick, Swords are Gods, Opportunity for Swords, Secret Trick is Tricky,
    - Time Egg, Time as A Kite, Eggs are Gods, Opportunity for Eggs, Secret as A Kite is Tricky,
    - Time Machines, Time Standards, Machines are Gods, Opportunity for Machines, Secret Standards is Tricky,
    - Time Monsters, Time Priests, Monsters are Gods, Opportunity for Monsters, Secret Priests are Tricky,
    - Time of Ages, Time Guides, Of Ages are Gods, Opportunity for of Ages, Secret Guides is Tricky,
    - Time of Pleasure, Time of Measurements, Of Pleasure are Gods, Opportunity for Pleasure, Secret of Measurements is Tricky,
    - Time State, Time Debauchery, States are Gods, Opportunity for States, Secret of Debauchery is Tricky,
    - Time Number, Time Greatness, Numbers are Gods, Opportunity for Numbers, Secret of Greatness is Tricky,
    - Time Time, Time Laziness, Times are Gods, Opportunity for Time, Secret of Laziness is Tricky,
    - Time Knowledge, Time Superficiality, Knowledges are Gods, Opportunity for Knowledge, Secret of Superficiality is Tricky
    - Time Yew, Time Weather, Yew are Gods, Opportunity for Yew, Secret of Weather is Tricky,
    - Time Abstracta, Time Prostitution, Abstract Gods, Opportunity for Abstractions, Secret of Prostitution is Tricky,
    - Time Exponents, Time Factors, Exponents are Gods, Opportunity for Exponents, Secret of Factors is Tricky,
    - Time Trumps, Time Signs, Trumps are Gods, Opportunity for Trumps, Secret of Signs is Tricky,
    - Time Soul. Time to Kill, Souls are Gods, Opportunity for Souls, Secret to Kill is Tricky,
    - Time of All Things, Time Disappointment, Of All Things are Gods, Opportunity for All Things, Secret of Disappointment is Tricky,
    - Time Entology, Time of Logic, Entologies are Gods, Opportunity for Entology, Secret of Logic is Tricky,
    - Time with Money, Time Promises, With Money are Gods, Opportunity for with Money, Secret of Promises is Tricky,
    - Time Reel, Time Standard, Reels are Gods, Opportunity for Reels, Secret Standard is Tricky,

- o Time Burgher, Time the Creeps, Burghers are Gods,
  Opportunity for Burghers, Secret O' the Creeps is Tricky,
- o Time Forever, Time Half-Life, Forevers are Gods,
  Opportunity for Forevers, Secret that Half-Lives are Tricky,
- o Time He's A Genius, Time Language, He's A Genius is Gods,
  Opportunity for He's A Genius, Secret of Language is Tricky,
- o Time on Earth, Time Nothing, On Earth is Gods, Opportunity
  for On Earth, Secret of Nothing is Tricky,

—Rumores

FUNDAMENTAL ARGUMENT OF THE SOUL

* Knowledge is necessary to describe a name.

* The title must have two parts for variation.

* The maximum poss variations with four
  parts is to conflict w/ title with the 2nd part,
  clarify with 3rd, and test with 4th.

* The resulting combinations are:
  Title of book = '[quality of X] [opp qualifier]'
  Soul of the book = 'If you [X] qualifier
  [subject of X and qualifier] [opp X clarified]'

Wisdom is intuitive spell-casting. [2-POLARITY]

- The insight here is that there is continuation between dimensions defined
  in terms of the (Sqroot of the total mathematical number theory categories
  -1) / 2, assuming an odd number of categories. With 25 categories, The
  properties of the dimension - 2 and the dimension +2 are the exclusive
  properties of the given dimension, implying a kind of coherent circularity.

625/32   D = 7

UNIVERSE 4: MAJOR ATTRIBUTES

TOE
1. MATH
2. ELEMENTS

FUNCTION
1. ELEMENTS
2. VARIATION

PSYCHIC
1. VARIATION
2. SPECIES

RESOURCES
1. SPECIES
2. MATH

PERPETUAL MOTION
1. WISH
2. MEANING

ENERGY
1. MEANING
2. LANGUAGE

ORGANIZ-ATION
1. LANGUAGE
2. SET

SUFFICIENCY
1. SET
2. WISH

ELEMENTS
1. T.O.E.
2. FUNCTION

VARIATION
1. FUNCTION
2. PSYCHIC

SPECIES
1. PSYCHIC
2. RESOURCES

MATH
1. RESOURCES
2. TOE

MEANING
1. PERPETUAL MOTION
2. ENERGY

LANGUAGE
1. ENERGY
2. ORGANIZ-ATION

SET
1. ORGANIZ-ATION
2. SUFFICIENCY

WISH
1. SUFFICIENCY
2. PERPETUAL MOTION

Dimensions are natures. [MULTI-PLURAL]

- This is the discovery that the Characteristica Universalis overlaps with the Unified Languages Theorem. It is also related to the expression of the disintegral in geometric space.
    - If something were not a category, it would have nothing.
    - If something could not stand, it would have a powerful base.
    - If something could not spread out, it would have length.
    - If something were incapable, it would swim in a soup.
    - If something were not alive, it could still be classified.
    - If something were not a system, it could still be called one.
    - If something had no substance, it would not exist.
    - If something was not abstract, it would exist.
    - If something was not organized, it would be a part of nature.
    - If something were not flagged, it would be noted.
        - Thus, everything that speaks a language must have one of these things, the first or the second.
        - And, so, everything that is missing one language is speaking another.
        - In the broadest sense, if we do not adhere to one modality, another modality applies.

—Observations on the Infinite Goldfish (…)

Efficient efficiency brings greater wisdom. [HYPER-FUNCTION]

- The realization here is that the TOE Thermo Diagram iterates between perpetual motion and magic, and between knowledge and immortality, when it comes to degrees of meta- or hyper-efficiency.

3.5-D T.O.E. THERMO DIAGRAM

IMMORTALITY **PERPETUAL MOTION**

OU   HIGH-Function   OU

     MECH

KNOW EVERYTHING

GREAT POWERS, LAW OF SURVIVAL   THERMO - 5   REACTIVE MECHANISMS

MAGICAL BRAINS, PROFOUND MEANING   THERMO -4   LIGHTER-THAN-AIR MECHANISMS
IMMUNITY, ABSTRACTION, MATERIALISM   SUPPORTED FLYING

HIGH EFF   THERMO -3   **HIGH DIFF**

POWERFUL DEMONS OF THE FUTURE   THERMO -2   SELF-POWERED FLYING

GOOD FORTUNE GOOD MEMORY   THERMO -1   MECHANICAL OVER-UNITY

WEAKNESS   THERMO 0   ABSTRACTIONS

MORTALITY   THERMO +1   OBJECTIVE KNOWLEDGE

DEADLY PARASITES   LANGS

LOW EFF   THERMO +2   **LOW DIFF**

EXTERMINATION   THERMO +3   IMMORTAL LANGS

DISEASE   THERMO +4   DRACONIAN NETWORKS

SACRIFICE   THERMO +5   ARCANE NETWORKS

UU   UU

KNOW   HIGH-Dimension   MECH

DEATH MAGIC   **KNOWLEDGE**

...

Unfailing presence is problematic problems. [POLISH]

- This is explained as the insight from Atheistic Theology proofs that perpetual motion is likely the real explanation for the attributes of God, e.g. it is a possible guess that what humans unconsciously mean by God is really perpetual motion machines. Therefore, the expansion of 'unfailing presence' e.g. eternal energy for problematic problems is the expanded equations for perpetual motion machines, specifically the variations which are compatible with the TOE.
  - Min Results = (Max Eff / 2) + Diff
  - Max Results = Min Eff + Diff
  - Min Eff = Results - Diff
  - Max Eff = (Min Results - Diff) X 2
  - Over-Unity = ((Max Results - Min Results) / (Max Eff / Min Eff)) X 100 (%)
  - Proportion of Smaller Unit = 1X
  - So far as objective elements, a value of 6.5 + the Function Number yields the number of components. Typical Function numbers are ordinal numbers of 1, 2, zero, -1, or -2.
  - Extra Mass < OU - 100%
  - Against Gravity Extra Mass < OU - 200%
  - No Flying when (Max Eff - Min Eff) >= 1/2 Max Eff.
  - Flying Machines Window = Max Results - Min Results
  - Flying Max Results = (Min Eff) <-- correct
  - Flying Min Results = (Max Eff / 2) <-- correct
  - Flying OU = (Max Results - Min Results) / (Max Eff - Min Eff) + 1 * 100 (%) + 100 for flying.
  - Standard Buoyancy Ratio = 1X
  - A theory of OU Flying: <u>Improved Balancing Balloons Theory</u>
  - Estimated Max OU of Planetoids = < (Phi / 2 + 1 * 100 =) 180.9% OU,
  - Max sustainable mass resistance to OU = <<0.809 X distance (Earth diameters). With an estimate saying Earth's max output is about 110% with rotation.
  - OU holds the key to matter.
  - Antigravity hold the key to the open set.

Nature bind is a self-solving problem. [SLIGHT]

- TOE --> 11 Laws of Thermo --> Importance of Difference --> Trinity Reunion (realization of importance of the three theories as variations on the TOE) --> Proof of Exponential Efficiency (Proof of Perfect Argument used with all three initial variations).
  - Proof of Exponential Efficiency (TOE)
    - Math is general.
    - General but incomplete is incoherent.

- If math is not comprehensive, comprehensive logic might be used.
- Comprehensive logic incorporates opposite poles spanning the largest possible distance, and therefore opposed diagonally.
- The model must also be advantageous to beat incoherent models, which in logic comparable to mathematics means having an exponentially-efficient advantage.
- An exponentially-efficient advantage is already created by rotating the diagonal opposites, creating two combinations for four categories.
- The simplest way to express the logic is Results (1,2,3…) = Eff + Difference, where results is the number of deductions and Efficiency can be taken as 1 for coherence or 3 for modularity of a square, and difference can be taken as 1 for oppositeness, or -1 for abstraction. In either case the output is two deductions.

o Proof of Exponential Efficiency (Perpetual Motion)
- Applications are specific.
- A mechanical model must be general.
- If applications are not specific, they must still express energy or they will not have efficiency.
- Since energy is expressed as efficiency, and what is needed is a general theory of mechanics (physics) in which energy is not constant, so exponents may be used to express this.
- Thus, what is called 'efficiency mechanics' has been said to involve differences in which exponential efficiency is created.
- It will most likely involve compound efficiencies.
- Assuming the general formula is the most useful, the simplest explanation is that it takes the form: Results = Eff (1,2,3…) + Difference.

o Proof of Exponential Efficiency (Function Spectrum)
- Unifying the general and specific involves unifying the abstract and material.
- The abstract is general because it is the TOE, and the material is general because it is the TOE.
- The unification of the abstract and general must include both.
- Since the theory involves exclusively coherence, which is unity, and perpetual motion, which is over-unity, it will be a theory of energy.
- Since both theories involve the TOE, it is also a fully abstract theory.

- The simplest explanation is that knowledge and energy are two opposite arms of the same Function Spectrum.
- Assuming the correct formula includes both the general and the specific, it can be written as: Results = Eff + Difference (1,2,3…)

—Proof of Exponential Efficiency (…)

Natural power is metaphysical semantics. [RARITIES]

- The most powerful connection here appears to be with NC Tree Theory, e.g. all of the below equations have infinite trees which mostly repeat (the repetitions can have different formulas than those mentioned here: these are just the 'primary TOE' style formulas within the sets. The larger sets are often vaguely similar to the disintegral, but may be completely different formulas than any of those below. An attempt at a complete list of them is developing at NC Tree Theory).
  - T.O.E.
    - KNOWLEDGE: Results (1,2,3…) = Eff + Difference
    - PERPETUAL MOTION: Results = Eff (1,2,3…) + Difference
    - FUNCTION SPECTRUM: Results = Eff + Difference (1,2,3…)
  - Anti-Theory:
    - Anti-Thing (1,2,3…) <= Difference - Efficiency
    - Anti-Thing <= Difference (1,2,3…) - Efficiency
    - Anti-Thing <= Difference - Efficiency (1,2,3…)
  - Efficiency:
    - Efficiency (1,2,3…) >= Results – Difference
    - Efficiency >= Results (1,2,3…) – Difference
    - Efficiency >= Results – Difference (1,2,3…)
  - Anti-Efficiency:
    - Anti-Efficiency (1,2,3…) <= Difference - Results
    - Anti-Efficiency <= Difference (1,2,3…) - Results
    - Anti-Efficiency <= Difference - Results (1,2,3…)
  - Difference:
    - Difference (1,2,3…) >= Results – Efficiency
    - Difference >= Results (1,2,3…) – Efficiency
    - Difference >= Results – Efficiency (1,2,3…)
  - Anti-Difference:
    - Anti-Difference (1,2,3…) <= Efficiency - Results
    - Anti-Difference <= Efficiency (1,2,3…) - Results
    - Anti-Difference <= Efficiency - Results (1,2,3…)
  - Forces:
    - # Forces (1,2,3…) = # Dimensions - # Antiforces
    - # Forces = # Dimensions (1,2,3…) - # Antiforces

- # Forces = # Dimensions - # Antiforces (1,2,3…)
  - Antiforces:
    - # Antiforces (1,2,3…) = # Dimensions - # Forces
    - # Antiforces = # Dimensions (1,2,3…) - # Forces
    - # Antiforces = # Dimensions - # Forces (1,2,3…)
  - Dimensions:
    - # Dimensions (1,2,3…) = # Forces + # Antiforces
    - # Dimensions = # Forces (1,2,3…) + # Antiforces
    - # Dimensions = # Forces + # Antiforces (1,2,3…)
  - Anti-Dimensions:
    - # Anti-Dimensions (1,2,3…) = # Antiforces - # Forces
    - # Anti-Dimensions = # Antiforces - # Forces (1,2,3…) +
    - # Anti-Dimensions = # Antiforces (1,2,3…) - # Forces
  - Disintegral:
    - Disintegral (1,2,3…) = Efficiency – Difference
    - Disintegral = Efficiency – Difference (1,2,3…)
    - Disintegral = Efficiency (1,2,3…) – Difference
  - Anti-Disintegral or Abstract Efficiency:
    - Results (1,2,3…) = Difference – Efficiency
    - Results = Diff (1,2,3…) – Efficiency
    - Results = -Diff – Efficiency (1,2,3…)
  - Super-Disintegral:
    - Super-Disintegral (1,2,3…) = Inf Eff – Inf Diff
    - Super-Disintegral = Inf Eff – Inf Diff (1,2,3…)
    - Super-Disintegral = Inf Eff (1,2,3…) - Inf Diff
  - Anti-Super-Disintegral:
    - Anti-Super-Disintegral (1,2,3…) = - (Inf Eff – Inf Diff)
    - Anti-Super-Disintegral = - (Inf Eff (1,2,3…) – Inf Diff)
    - Anti-Super-Disintegral = - (Inf Eff – Inf Diff (1,2,3…))
  - Min Results:
    - Min Results (1,2,3…) = (Max Eff / 2) + Diff
    - Min Results = (Max Eff (1,2,3…) / 2) + Diff
    - Min Results = (Max Eff / 2) + Diff (1,2,3…)
  - Max Results:
    - Max Results (1,2,3…) = Min Eff + Diff
    - Max Results = Min Eff (1,2,3…) + Diff
    - Max Results = Min Eff + Diff (1,2,3…)
  - Min Efficiency:
    - Min Eff (1,2,3…) = Results - Diff
    - Min Eff = Results (1,2,3…) - Diff
    - Min Eff = Results - Diff (1,2,3…)
  - Max Efficiency:
    - Max Eff (1,2,3…) = (Min Results - Diff) X 2

- Max Eff = (Min Results (1,2,3…) - Diff) X 2
- Max Eff = (Min Results - Diff (1,2,3…)) X 2
  - Flying Max Results
    - Flying Max Results (1,2,3…) = (Min Eff) + 2 Eff - 1
    - Flying Max Results = (Min Eff (1,2,3…)) + 2 Eff - 1
    - Flying Max Results = (Min Eff) + 2 Eff (1,2,3…) - 1
  - Flying Min Results
    - Flying Min Results (1,2,3…) = (Max Eff / 2) + 2 Eff - 1
    - Flying Min Results = (Max Eff (1,2,3…) / 2) + 2 Eff - 1
    - Flying Min Results = (Max Eff / 2) + 2 Eff (1,2,3…) - 1

Diabolical genius is a paradoxical brain. [MANIFOLDS]

- One guess is this is given by 'skip, madness, skip', a key element of the Coherent Brain. A development of this gives a kind of coherent magical process which integrates coherence theory and occult properties. This was a basis for the reduction of the functional categories of the TOE to 11 categories, suggesting an exciting integration between the TOE and the 11 Alternate Systems (at some point).
  - Standard Logic:
    - Descriptive model.
    - Continuation of the logic.
    - Description of a finite infinite.
    - Exponentiation of some external.
  - Coherence:
    - Expression of a complete model.
    - Containment of the model.
    - Description of the absolute.
    - Exponential efficiency.
    - The sense of fulfillment (completeness). Obviously more beneficial than before.
    - Containment, which is to say, continuing reward, possibly more advanced than serotonin.
    - The absolute, which is to say, ultimate, or a scientific equivalent (perhaps).
    - A principle of exponential efficiency, which means an enhanced effect of the above.
    - Coherence is a better model for chemical rewards than traditional logic. —Coherence and Chemical Rewards

A HISTORICAL MODEL OF DEVELOPMENTAL COHERENCE

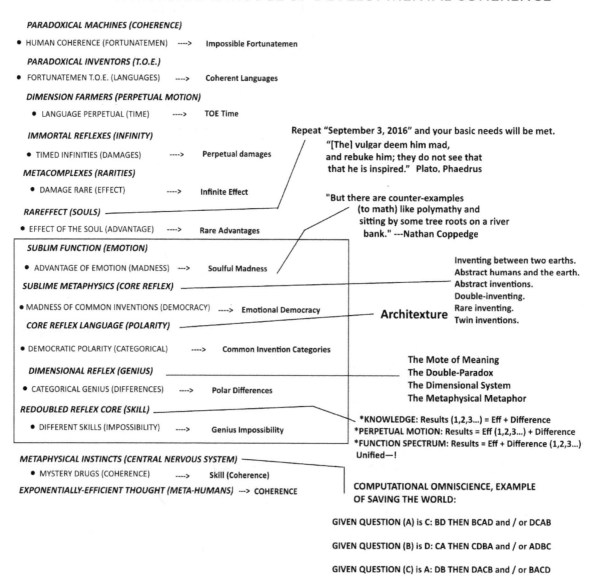

PARADOXICAL MACHINES (COHERENCE)

● HUMAN COHERENCE (FORTUNATEMEN)   ---->   Impossible Fortunatemen

PARADOXICAL INVENTORS (T.O.E.)

● FORTUNATEMEN T.O.E. (LANGUAGES)   ---->   Coherent Languages

DIMENSION FARMERS (PERPETUAL MOTION)

● LANGUAGE PERPETUAL (TIME)   ---->   TOE Time

IMMORTAL REFLEXES (INFINITY)

● TIMED INFINITIES (DAMAGES)   ---->   Perpetual damages

METACOMPLEXES (RARITIES)

● DAMAGE RARE (EFFECT)   ---->   Infinite Effect

RAREFFECT (SOULS)

● EFFECT OF THE SOUL (ADVANTAGE)   ---->   Rare Advantages

SUBLIM FUNCTION (EMOTION)

● ADVANTAGE OF EMOTION (MADNESS)   --->   Soulful Madness

SUBLIME METAPHYSICS (CORE REFLEX)

● MADNESS OF COMMON INVENTIONS (DEMOCRACY)   ---->   Emotional Democracy

CORE REFLEX LANGUAGE (POLARITY)

● DEMOCRATIC POLARITY (CATEGORICAL)   ---->   Common Invention Categories

DIMENSIONAL REFLEX (GENIUS)

● CATEGORICAL GENIUS (DIFFERENCES)   ---->   Polar Differences

REDOUBLED REFLEX CORE (SKILL)

● DIFFERENT SKILLS (IMPOSSIBILITY)   ---->   Genius Impossibility

METAPHYSICAL INSTINCTS (CENTRAL NERVOUS SYSTEM)

● MYSTERY DRUGS (COHERENCE)   ---->   Skill (Coherence)

EXPONENTIALLY-EFFICIENT THOUGHT (META-HUMANS) ---> COHERENCE

Repeat "September 3, 2016" and your basic needs will be met.

"[The] vulgar deem him mad,
and rebuke him; they do not see that
that he is inspired." Plato. Phaedrus

"But there are counter-examples
(to math) like polymathy and
sitting by some tree roots on a river
bank." ---Nathan Coppedge

Inventing between two earths.
Abstract humans and the earth.
Abstract inventions.
Double-inventing.
Rare inventing.
Twin inventions.

Architexture

The Mote of Meaning
The Double-Paradox
The Dimensional System
The Metaphysical Metaphor

*KNOWLEDGE: Results (1,2,3...) = Eff + Difference
*PERPETUAL MOTION: Results = Eff (1,2,3...) + Difference
*FUNCTION SPECTRUM: Results = Eff + Difference (1,2,3...)
Unified—!

COMPUTATIONAL OMNISCIENCE, EXAMPLE
OF SAVING THE WORLD:

GIVEN QUESTION (A) is C: BD THEN BCAD and / or DCAB

GIVEN QUESTION (B) is D: CA THEN CDBA and / or ADBC

GIVEN QUESTION (C) is A: DB THEN DACB and / or BACD

GIVEN QUESTION (D) is B: AC THEN ABDC and / or CBDA

. . .

[March 31, 2022] INSIGHT BLOCK 7

Good combination is a luxury platform. [SKRIMS]

- This may be seen as a system which prefers perpetual motion above other results. What is good and highest is analogous to perpetual motion. Corresponding to the specific category of the Shadowy Occlusion like perpetual motion is a founding category of the NC Tree Theory and TOE, Immortality might be used to explain the ultimate of the Luxury Platform of Consciousness sometimes associated with Immortality (Category 14 or 15) and Difference (Category 23 or 24).
    - 0. Immortal Substance (Motto: "It's impossibly real")
    - 1. Immortally Marvelous (Motto: "It's marvelous, so it seems impossible")
    - 2. Eternal Immortality (Motto: "If it keeps running, it's literally a miracle")
    - 3. Explanation of Immortality (Motto: "These perpetual motion machines take us back to infinity")
    - 4. Diagrammatic Immortality (Motto: "We have a diagram, now it is back to the old perpetual motion machines")
    - 5. Immortal Analysis (Motto: "We are analyzing, now it is back to the diagrams")
    - 6. Coherent Immortality (Motto: "Back to analyzing, which will result in visual diagrams")
    - 7. Information Immortality (Motto: "There is coherence back there somewhere")
    - 8. Paradigmatic Immortality (Motto: "Information immortality has become archaic")
    - 9. Content Immortality (Motto: "Now that we have content, we can focus on information")
    - 10. Dimensional Immortality (Motto: "We have multiple dimensions, then we can create content")
    - 11. Immortal Meaning (Motto: "We found something meaningful and meaning has dimensions")
    - 12. Immortal Singularity (Motto: "We have thought of something singular. It might have meaning!")
    - 13. Immortal Soothing (Motto: "There is something soothing. What singular sense emerges from it?")
    - 14. Immortal Sublimata (Motto: "What is good about it if it does not sooth us?")
    - 15. Immortal Subtlimata (Motto: "Now that it is realized, so subtle it seems, it might be sublime.")

THEORY OF ANYTHING MATHEMATICS

UNIVERSE 20   D = NEG1
#8 MEANING 5/32
RESULTS= NEG INF,
EFF= NEG INF,
EFF= RESULTS
DIFF= 0

UNIVERSE 21:   D= NEG2
#9 SINGULAR FRINGE
RESULTS= NEG INF,
EFF= NEG FIN.
DIFF = RESULTS

UNIVERSE 22: D=NEG3
#10 SINGULAR
CATEGORIES
RESULTS= NEG INF,
EFF = 0,
DIFF = RESULTS

UNIVERSE 23: D = NEG4
#11 SOOTHING
LUXURIES
RESULT = NEG INF,
EFF= FIN,
DIFF= RESULTS

X UNIVERSE 24   D = NEG5
#12 SUBLIMISM:
VARIATIONS
RESULTS= NEG INF,
EFF= INF,
DIFF= IMPOSSIBLE

UNIVERSE 15   D = 2
#3 LANGUAGE NOTICES
X   INFORMATION
RESULTS= NEG FIN,
EFF= NEG INF,
DIFF = INF

UNIVERSE 16:   D = 0
#4 TIMED EFFECTS
RESULTS = NEG FIN
EFF = NEG FIN
DIFF = -(EFF)+RESULTS

UNIVERSE 17:   D = 0
#5 DAMAGE
RESULTS = NEG FIN
EFF = 0
DIFF = RESULTS

UNIVERSE 18:   D = 0
#6 EFFECTS
RESULTS = NEG FIN
EFF = FIN
DIFF = NEGEFF+RESULTS

UNIVERSE 19   D = 1
#7 DIMENSIONS:
CONTENT GENERATORS
RESULTS= NEG FIN,
X   EFF= INF,
DIFF= NEG INF

UNIVERSE 10 D = 4
#23 NOTICE COHERENCE
RESULTS= 0,
EFF= NEG INF,
DIFF =   INF

UNIVERSE 11:   D = 0
#24 SKILLS
RESULTS = ZERO
EFF = NEG FIN
DIFF =FIN

UNIVERSE 12:   D = 0
#25 NEUTRALS
RESULTS = ZERO
EFF = ZERO
DIFF = ZERO

UNIVERSE
#1 COMPLEX BODIES   D = 0
RESULTS = AVG ZERO
EFF = FIN
DIFF = AVG - EFF

UNIVERSE 14   D = 3
#2 HEROIC
INFORMATION
RESULTS 0,
EFF= INF,
DIFF= NEG INF

UNIVERSE 5   D = 6
X #18 RARITIES
RESULTS= FIN,
EFF= NEG INF.
DIFF = INF

UNIVERSE 6:   D = 0
#19 SOULS
RESULTS = FIN
EFF = NEG FIN
DIFF = -(EFF) + RESULTS

UNIVERSE 7:   D = 0
#20 EMOTION
RESULTS = FIN
EFF = 0
DIFF = RESULTS

UNIVERSE 8:   D = 0
#21 CORES
RESULTS = FIN
EFF= FIN
DIFF =RESULTS - EFF

UNIVERSE 9   D = 5
X #22 LIMIT FUNCTIONS
RESULTS= FIN,
EFF= INF,
DIFF= NEG INF

X UNIVERSE 0 D = 11
#13 IMPOSSIBLY REAL
RESULTS= INF,
EFF= NEG INF,
DIFF= IMPOSSIBLE

UNIVERSE 1 D = 10
#14 IMMORTAL WISHES
RESULTS= INF,
EFF= NEG FIN
DIFF= RESULTS

UNIVERSE 2   D = 9
#15 RATIONAIRE
RESULTS=INF,
EFF= 0,
DIFF= RESULTS

UNIVERSE 3   D = 8
#16 PERPETUAL MOTION
MACHINES
RESULTS= INF
EFF= FIN,
DIFF= RESULTS

UNIVERSE 4 D=7
#17 DIAGRAM'S
DERIGATIVE
RESULTS= INF,
EFF= RESULTS
DIFF= 0

Free and must remain non-proprietary, Nathan Larkin Coppedge

Mode of immortality is a sublime reality. [D-LEVELS]

Dynamic meaning is polar opposites. [WINDFALLS]

- This may be associated with the 'Shadowy Occlusion' a discovery relating to polar opposites which collapses the magical and immortal into a single perhaps simpler 'shadow side of things'. This insight may help magic as it directs the remaining categories into an ascending and descending singular idea, and is potentially singularized also by the collapse of the shadow side. Oddly, this difference has been associated with genders and is a development of difference theory which is likely important for all constituent theories of the TOE. It may also anticipate the formation of multiple theories equivalent to the the TOE Diagram, the 11 Laws of Thermodynamics, the TOE Thermo Diagram, and the Shadowy Occlusion.

THE SHADOWY OCCLUSION

SUBLIME POTENTIAL
TIMELESS & PERFECT
ENDLESS TRAVERSAL
IDYLLIC TRAVELLERS
FORMS VOLITIO
WEAK ABSTRACTIONS
TRUE KNOWLEDGE
RELIGIOUS LANGUAGE
DEAD LANGUAGES
INFECTED MAGIC
SACRIFICE PRINCIPLE

THE SHADOW SPECTRUM
EFFICIENCY OR DIFFERENCE
IMMORTALITY OR MAGIC

THE FUNCTION SPECTRUM
PERPETUAL MOTION OR
KNOWLEDGE, POSITIVE
OR NEGATIVE

**THE SHADOW ONLY WANTS
TO BE COMPATIBLE**

Meaningful meaning is the second system. [VERBS]

- Not sure of the exact meaning of this, but Verb Theory has been completed to some degree:
    - -5 Archaic Networks
    - 1-d, 1 result = -5 + (D ^ 1) - 0.5 = -4.5 Verbs Losses
    - 1-d, 2 results = -5 + (D ^ 2) - 0.5 = -4.5 Verbs Losses
    - 1-d, 3 results = -5 + (D ^ 3) - 0.5 = -4.5 Verbs Losses

- o 1-d, 4 results = -5 + (D ^ 4) - 0.5 = -4.5 Verbs Losses
- o 2-d, 1 result = -5 + (D ^ 1) - 0.5 = -3.5 Verbs
- o 2-d, 2 results = -5 + (D ^ 2) - 0.5 = -1.5 Verbs Dead-end
- o 2-d, 3 results = -5 + (D ^ 3) - 0.5 = 2.5 Verbs (positive) Immortal
- o 2-d, 4 results = -5 + (D ^ 4) - 0.5 = 10.5 Verbs (positive)
- o 3-d, 1 result = -5 + (D ^ 1) - 0.5 = -2.5 Verbs (negative) Impossibility
- o 3-d, 2 results = -5 + (D ^ 2) - 0.5 = 3.5 Verbs (positive)
- o 3-d, 3 results = -5 + (D ^ 3) - 0.5 = 21.5 Verbs
- o 3-d, 4 results = -5 + (D ^ 4) - 0.5 = 75.5 Verbs
- o 4-d, 1 result = -5 + (D ^ 1) - 0.5 = -1.5 Verbs (negative)
- o 4-d, 2 results = -5 + (D ^ 2) - 0.5 = 10.5 Verbs (positive)
- o 4-d, 3 results = -5 + (D ^ 3) - 0.5 = 58.5 Verbs
- o 4-d, 4 results = -5 + (D ^ 4) - 0.5 = 250.5 Verbs
- o -4 Draconian Networks
- o 1-d, 1 result = -4 + (D ^ 1) - 0.5 = -3.5 Verbs
- o 1-d, 2 results = -4 + (D ^ 2) - 0.5 = -3.5 Verbs
- o 1-d, 3 results = -4 + (D ^ 3) - 0.5 = -3.5 Verbs
- o 1-d, 4 results = -4 + (D ^ 4) - 0.5 = -3.5 Verbs
- o 2-d, 1 result = -4 + (D ^ 1) - 0.5 = -2.5 Verbs Impossibility
- o 2-d, 2 results = -4 + (D ^ 2) - 0.5 = -0.5 Verbs Abstraction
- o 2-d, 3 results = -4 + (D ^ 3) - 0.5 = 3.5 Verbs
- o 2-d, 4 results = -4 + (D ^ 4) - 0.5 = 11.5 Verbs
- o 3-d, 1 result = -4 + (D ^ 1) - 0.5 = -1.5 Verbs (negative) Dead-end
- o 3-d, 2 results = -4 + (D ^ 2) - 0.5 = 4.5 Verbs (positive)
- o 3-d, 3 results = -4 + (D ^ 3) - 0.5 = 22.5 Verbs
- o 3-d, 4 results = -4 + (D ^ 4) - 0.5 = 76.5 Verbs
- o 4-d, 1 result = -4 + (D ^ 1) - 0.5 = -0.5 Verbs (negative) Abstraction
- o 4-d, 2 results = -4 + (D ^ 2) - 0.5 = 11.5 Verbs (positive)
- o 4-d, 3 results = -4 + (D ^ 3) - 0.5 = 59.5 Verbs
- o 4-d, 4 results = -4 + (D ^ 4) - 0.5 = 251.5 Verbs
- o -3 Immortal Language
- o 1-d, 1 result = -3 + (D ^ 1) - 0.5 = -2.5 Verbs Impossibility
- o 1-d, 2 results = -3 + (D ^ 2) - 0.5 = -2.5 Verbs Impossibility
- o 1-d, 3 results = -3 + (D ^ 3) - 0.5 = -2.5 Verbs Impossibility
- o 1-d, 4 results = -3 + (D ^ 4) - 0.5 = -2.5 Verbs Impossibility
- o 2-d, 1 result = -3 + (D ^ 1) - 0.5 = -1.5 Verbs Dead-end
- o 2-d, 2 results = -3 + (D ^ 2) - 0.5 = +0.5 Verbs Items
- o 2-d, 3 results = -3 + (D ^ 3) - 0.5 = 4.5 Verbs Generation
- o 2-d, 4 results = -3 + (D ^ 4) - 0.5 = 12.5 Verbs
- o 3-d, 1 result = -3 + (D ^ 1) - 0.5 = -0.5 Verbs (negative) Abstraction
- o 3-d, 2 results = -3 + (D ^ 2) - 0.5 = 5.5 Verbs (positive) Eternal Time
- o 3-d, 3 results = -3 + (D ^ 3) - 0.5 = 23.5 Verbs Time-Travel
- o 3-d, 4 results = -3 + (D ^ 4) - 0.5 = 77.5 Verbs

- 4-d, 1 result = -3 + (D ^ 1) - 0.5 = +0.5 Verbs Items
- 4-d, 2 results = -3 + (D ^ 2) - 0.5 = 12.5 Verbs (positive)
- 4-d, 3 results = -3 + (D ^ 3) - 0.5 = 60.5 Verbs
- 4-d, 4 results = -3 + (D ^ 4) - 0.5 = 252.5 Verbs
- -2 Language
- 1-d, 1 result = -2 + (D ^ 1) - 0.5 = -1.5 Verbs Dead-end
- 1-d, 2 results = -2 + (D ^ 2) - 0.5 = -1.5 Verbs Dead-end
- 1-d, 3 results = -2 + (D ^ 3) - 0.5 = -1.5 Verbs Dead-end
- 1-d, 4 results = -2 + (D ^ 4) - 0.5 = -1.5 Verbs Dead-end
- 2-d, 1 result = -2 + (D ^ 1) - 0.5 = -0.5 Verbs Abstraction
- 2-d, 2 results = -2 + (D ^ 2) - 0.5 = +1.5 Verbs Perpetual motion
- 2-d, 3 results = -2 + (D ^ 3) - 0.5 = 5.5 Verbs
- 2-d, 4 results = -2 + (D ^ 4) - 0.5 = 13.5 Verbs
- 3-d, 1 result = -2 + (D ^ 1) - 0.5 = +0.5 Verbs Items
- 3-d, 2 results = -2 + (D ^ 2) - 0.5 = 6.5 Verbs
- 3-d, 3 results = -2 + (D ^ 3) - 0.5 = 24.5 Verbs
- 3-d, 4 results = -2 + (D ^ 4) - 0.5 = 78.5 Verbs
- 4-d, 1 result = -2 + (D ^ 1) - 0.5 = 1.5 Verbs Perpetual motion
- 4-d, 2 results = -2 + (D ^ 2) - 0.5 = 13.5 Verbs
- 4-d, 3 results = -2 + (D ^ 3) - 0.5 = 61.5 Verbs
- 4-d, 4 results = -2 + (D ^ 4) - 0.5 = 253.5 Verbs
- -1 Knowledge
- 1-d, 1 result = -1 + (D ^ 1) - 0.5 = -0.5 Verbs Abstraction
- 1-d, 2 results = -1 + (D ^ 2) - 0.5 = -0.5 Verbs Abstraction
- 1-d, 3 results = -1 + (D ^ 3) - 0.5 = -0.5 Verbs Abstraction
- 1-d, 4 results = -1 + (D ^ 4) - 0.5 = -0.5 Verbs Abstraction
- 2-d, 1 result = -1 + (D ^ 1) - 0.5 = 0.5 Verbs (positive) Items
- 2-d, 2 results = -1 + (D ^ 2) - 0.5 = 2.5 Verbs Immortal
- 2-d, 3 results = -1 + (D ^ 3) - 0.5 = 6.5 Verbs
- 2-d, 4 results = -1 + (D ^ 4) - 0.5 = 14.5 Verbs
- 3-d, 1 result = -1 + (D ^ 1) - 0.5 = 1.5 Verbs Perpetual motion
- 3-d, 2 results = -1 + (D ^ 2) - 0.5 = 7.5 Verbs
- 3-d, 3 results = -1 + (D ^ 3) - 0.5 = 25.5 Verbs
- 3-d, 4 results = -1 + (D ^ 4) - 0.5 = 79.5 Verbs
- 4-d, 1 result = -1 + (D ^ 1) - 0.5 = 2.5 Verbs
- 4-d, 2 results = -1 + (D ^ 2) - 0.5 = 14.5 Verbs
- 4-d, 3 results = -1 + (D ^ 3) - 0.5 = 62.5 Verbs
- 4-d, 4 results = -1 + (D ^ 4) - 0.5 = 254.5 Verbs
- 0 Ordinary
- 1-d, 1 result = 0 + (D ^ 1) - 0.5 = 0.5 Verbs Items
- 1-d, 2 results = 0 + (D ^ 2) - 0.5 = 0.5 Verbs Items
- 1-d, 3 results = 0 + (D ^ 3) - 0.5 = 0.5 Verbs Items
- 1-d, 4 results = 0 + (D ^ 4) - 0.5 = 0.5 Verbs Items
- 2-d, 1 result = 0 + (D ^ 1) - 0.5 = 1.5 Verbs Perpetual motion
- 2-d, 2 results = 0 + (D ^ 2) - 0.5 = 3.5 Verbs
- 2-d, 3 results = 0 + (D ^ 3) - 0.5 = 7.5 Verbs
- 2-d, 4 results = 0 + (D ^ 4) - 0.5 = 15.5 Verbs
- 3-d, 1 result = 0 + (D ^ 1) - 0.5 = 2.5 Verbs Immortal

- 3-d, 2 results = 0 + (D ^ 2) - 0.5 = 8.5 Verbs
- 3-d, 3 results = 0 + (D ^ 3) - 0.5 = 26.5 Verbs
- 3-d, 4 results = 0 + (D ^ 4) - 0.5 = 80.5 Verbs
- 4-d, 1 result = 0 + (D ^ 1) - 0.5 = 3.5 Verbs
- 4-d, 2 results = 0 + (D ^ 2) - 0.5 = 15.5 Verbs
- 4-d, 3 results = 0 + (D ^ 3) - 0.5 = 63.5 Verbs
- 4-d, 4 results = 0 + (D ^ 4) - 0.5 = 255.5 Verbs
- 1 Perpetual Motion
- 1-d, 1 result = 1 + (D ^ 1) - 0.5 = 1.5 Verbs Perpetual motion
- 1-d, 2 results = 1 + (D ^ 2) - 0.5 = 1.5 Verbs Perpetual motion
- 1-d, 3 results = 1 + (D ^ 3) - 0.5 = 1.5 Verbs Perpetual motion
- 1-d, 4 results = 1 + (D ^ 4) - 0.5 = 1.5 Verbs Perpetual motion
- 2-d, 1 result = 1 + (D ^ 1) - 0.5 = 2.5 Verbs Immortal
- 2-d, 2 results = 1 + (D ^ 2) - 0.5 = 4.5 Verbs Generation
- 2-d, 3 results = 1 + (D ^ 3) - 0.5 = 8.5 Verbs
- 2-d, 4 results = 1 + (D ^ 4) - 0.5 = 16.5 Verbs
- 3-d, 1 result = 1 + (D ^ 1) - 0.5 = 3.5 Verbs 1:1 machine with no mass
- 3-d, 2 results = 1 + (D ^ 2) - 0.5 = 9.5 Verbs 1:1 machine with added mass
- 3-d, 3 results = 1 + (D ^ 3) - 0.5 = 27.5 Verbs 2:1 machine
- 3-d, 4 results = 1 + (D ^ 4) - 0.5 = 81.5 Verbs 3:1 machine
- 4-d, 1 result = 1 + (D ^ 1) - 0.5 = 4.5 Verbs
- 4-d, 2 results = 1 + (D ^ 2) - 0.5 = 16.5 Verbs
- 4-d, 3 results = 1 + (D ^ 3) - 0.5 = 64.5 Verbs
- 4-d, 4 results = 1 + (D ^ 4) - 0.5 = 256.5 Verbs
- 2 Perpetual Motion Flying Machines
- 1-d, 1 result = 2 + (D ^ 1) - 0.5 = 2.5 Verbs Immortal
- 1-d, 2 results = 2 + (D ^ 2) - 0.5 = 2.5 Verbs Immortal
- 1-d, 3 results = 2 + (D ^ 3) - 0.5 = 2.5 Verbs Immortal
- 1-d, 4 results = 2 + (D ^ 4) - 0.5 = 2.5 Verbs Immortal
- 2-d, 1 result = 2 + (D ^ 1) - 0.5 = 3.5 Verbs
- 2-d, 2 results = 2 + (D ^ 2) - 0.5 = 5.5 Verbs
- 2-d, 3 results = 2 + (D ^ 3) - 0.5 = 9.5 Verbs
- 2-d, 4 results = 2 + (D ^ 4) - 0.5 = 17.5 Verbs
- 3-d, 1 result = 2 + (D ^ 1) - 0.5 = 4.5 Verbs Generation
- 3-d, 2 results = 2 + (D ^ 2) - 0.5 = 10.5 Verbs
- 3-d, 3 results = 2 + (D ^ 3) - 0.5 = 28.5 Verbs
- 3-d, 4 results = 2 + (D ^ 4) - 0.5 = 82.5 Verbs
- 4-d, 1 result = 2 + (D ^ 1) - 0.5 = 5.5 Verbs
- 4-d, 2 results = 2 + (D ^ 2) - 0.5 = 17.5 Verbs
- 4-d, 3 results = 2 + (D ^ 3) - 0.5 = 65.5 Verbs
- 4-d, 4 results = 2 + (D ^ 4) - 0.5 = 257.5 Verbs
- 3 4-d Immortals
- 1-d, 1 result = 3 + (D ^ 1) - 0.5 = 3.5 Verbs
- 1-d, 2 results = 3 + (D ^ 2) - 0.5 = 3.5 Verbs
- 1-d, 3 results = 3 + (D ^ 3) - 0.5 = 3.5 Verbs
- 1-d, 4 results = 3 + (D ^ 4) - 0.5 = 3.5 Verbs
- 2-d, 1 result = 3 + (D ^ 1) - 0.5 = 4.5 Verbs Generation

- 2-d, 2 results = $3 + (D \wedge 2) - 0.5 = 6.5$ Verbs
- 2-d, 3 results = $3 + (D \wedge 3) - 0.5 = 10.5$ Verbs
- 2-d, 4 results = $3 + (D \wedge 4) - 0.5 = 18.5$ Verbs
- 3-d, 1 result = $3 + (D \wedge 1) - 0.5 = 5.5$ Verbs
- 3-d, 2 results = $3 + (D \wedge 2) - 0.5 = 11.5$ Verbs
- 3-d, 3 results = $3 + (D \wedge 3) - 0.5 = 29.5$ Verbs
- 3-d, 4 results = $3 + (D \wedge 4) - 0.5 = 83.5$ Verbs
- 4-d, 1 result = $3 + (D \wedge 1) - 0.5 = 6.5$ Verbs
- 4-d, 2 results = $3 + (D \wedge 2) - 0.5 = 18.5$ Verbs
- 4-d, 3 results = $3 + (D \wedge 3) - 0.5 = 66.5$ Verbs
- 4-d, 4 results = $3 + (D \wedge 4) - 0.5 = 258.5$ Verbs
- 4 5-d Immortals
- 1-d, 1 result = $4 + (D \wedge 1) - 0.5 = 4.5$ Verbs Generation
- 1-d, 2 results = $4 + (D \wedge 2) - 0.5 = 4.5$ Verbs Generation
- 1-d, 3 results = $4 + (D \wedge 3) - 0.5 = 4.5$ Verbs Generation
- 1-d, 4 results = $4 + (D \wedge 4) - 0.5 = 4.5$ Verbs Generation
- 2-d, 1 result = $4 + (D \wedge 1) - 0.5 = 5.5$ Verbs
- 2-d, 2 results = $4 + (D \wedge 2) - 0.5 = 7.5$ Verbs
- 2-d, 3 results = $4 + (D \wedge 3) - 0.5 = 11.5$ Verbs
- 2-d, 4 results = $4 + (D \wedge 4) - 0.5 = 19.5$ Verbs
- 3-d, 1 result = $4 + (D \wedge 1) - 0.5 = 6.5$ Verbs
- 3-d, 2 results = $4 + (D \wedge 2) - 0.5 = 12.5$ Verbs
- 3-d, 3 results = $4 + (D \wedge 3) - 0.5 = 30.5$ Verbs
- 3-d, 4 results = $4 + (D \wedge 4) - 0.5 = 84.5$ Verbs
- 4-d, 1 result = $4 + (D \wedge 1) - 0.5 = 7.5$ Verbs
- 4-d, 2 results = $4 + (D \wedge 2) - 0.5 = 19.5$ Verbs
- 4-d, 3 results = $4 + (D \wedge 3) - 0.5 = 67.5$ Verbs
- 4-d, 4 results = $4 + (D \wedge 4) - 0.5 = 259.5$ Verbs
- 5 6-d Immortals
- 1-d, 1 result = $5 + (D \wedge 1) - 0.5 = 5.5$ Verbs
- 1-d, 2 results = $5 + (D \wedge 2) - 0.5 = 5.5$ Verbs
- 1-d, 3 results = $5 + (D \wedge 3) - 0.5 = 5.5$ Verbs
- 1-d, 4 results = $5 + (D \wedge 4) - 0.5 = 5.5$ Verbs
- 2-d, 1 result = $5 + (D \wedge 1) - 0.5 = 6.5$ Verbs
- 2-d, 2 results = $5 + (D \wedge 2) - 0.5 = 8.5$ Verbs
- 2-d, 3 results = $5 + (D \wedge 3) - 0.5 = 12.5$ Verbs
- 2-d, 4 results = $5 + (D \wedge 4) - 0.5 = 20.5$ Verbs
- 3-d, 1 result = $5 + (D \wedge 1) - 0.5 = 7.5$ Verbs
- 3-d, 2 results = $5 + (D \wedge 2) - 0.5 = 13.5$ Verbs
- 3-d, 3 results = $5 + (D \wedge 3) - 0.5 = 31.5$ Verbs
- 3-d, 4 results = $5 + (D \wedge 4) - 0.5 = 85.5$ Verbs
- 4-d, 1 result = $5 + (D \wedge 1) - 0.5 = 8.5$ Verbs
- 4-d, 2 results = $5 + (D \wedge 2) - 0.5 = 20.5$ Verbs
- 4-d, 3 results = $5 + (D \wedge 3) - 0.5 = 68.5$ Verbs
- 4-d, 4 results = $5 + (D \wedge 4) - 0.5 = 260.5$ Verbs

[End of March 31, 2022]

April 1, 2022: Preverbs: Life is not overpowering. Life is sympathetic. Enjourney. Something will come of it.

April 2, 2022: For "DARPA Prophecies":

- Robots just want to be robots. XXX robots (robots may lead to extinction otherwise as they are inherently non-genetic, and genes concern survival).
- Quantum computers can be beat by conventional computers or a new invention ('Linnaean stem problem'). XXX quantum computers or expect technology to slow down.
- Education requires stimulation, fairness, and completeness. Coherence is the simplest, most fair-minded way to stimulate students. XXX incoherent approach to education or expect stupider students.
- Drugs benefit from coherent approaches. XXX serotonin cycle approach or expect harder drugs and more depression.
- Students are learning about mathematics. XXX non-dimensional (non-coherently-organized) approaches or expect a reversal against mathematics.

April 5, 2022: Meaningful constants anyone? Possible idea of the year, 2022

April 5, 2022: The Caravenserie / The Caravansary:

They could have 15 kinds of pepper. Those authentic people. I bet they did. They could learn Chinese the hard way, and it would be like real Chinese. Those authentic people.

April 5, 2022: How to Escape the Gladiatorial Arena

Escape the Gladiatorial Arena

- Meaning constants.
- Intuition pumps.
- Consciousness is plausibly a natural phenomenon. —Have any modern philosophers posed any significant life questions within the last 100 years?
- The Caravanserie / The Caravansary (...)
- Pichoo out of there.
- Bad dates.
- Start chuckling to yourself.

April 6, 2022: Escher Technology

Escher Rifling for faster shots: 1.1025 percent degrees need not be curved—An Argument Defending the Escher Machine

Escher Breasts: 35.1059

April 6, 2022 View of Eastern Philosophy:

Awakenment,

Forsakenment,

Astonishment,

Atunement

APRIL 6, 2022: Healing scars: The second heart is second search, turmeric and such. Feel scar lengthwise with index finger if it doesn't hurt, think of elongating scar. Repeat: Gloaming, snake bitre, gloaming, snake bitre, gloaming, snake bitre... Repeat.

APRIL 6, 2022: The Exclusives, an initial chemical pattern of immortality:

Stand away, and behold! This is after discovering an ability for Magical Healing of Scars

Sublime 2-Method:

PICK ONLY SUBLIME TERMS — IGNORE IF SUSPICIOUS

Sublime 3-Method

EXPLORE EXAMPLES	—	BEST EXAMPLES	—	ARRANGE BY COHERENT NUMBERS

Logic ---> Quantify ---> Define Set ---> History

SUBLIME 5-METHOD
(1) You want to work on the best thing --->
(2) Then Procedure (disorganized) --->
(3) Then Best Quotes (ideas) --->
(4) Then ideas (black swans) --->
(5) Then organize (TOE)

- **Insight: Computing --> Neurology --> Awakening**
- **Advice: Advanced Technical --> New logic --> Computing**
- **Meditation: Calculus --> Missing socks --> Advanced technical**
- **Sight: Unique people --> Genius --> Calculus**
- **Possibility: Strategy --> Language --> Unique People**
- **Ideas: Time --> Philosophy --> Strategy**—Immortality Drug Research (...)

2022–04–07: The key here is to notice fantasy may cause depression or it may not, but that is what's on people's minds. If information, like writing, cannot transform into fantasy, it is likely that science fiction is a dead end. Litmus test.

HISTORYPLOT CREATIVITY

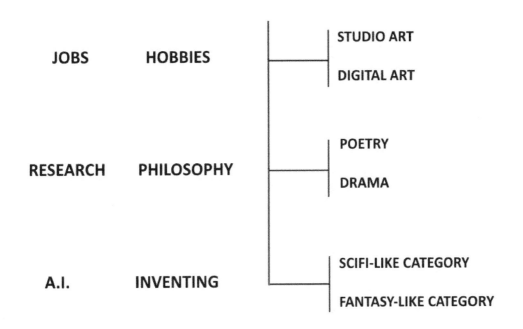

2022-04-10: SPECIES SURVIVAL EQUATION

D = Spatial dimensions, also called conceptual dimensions.

TC = Total Categories (Mathematical number theory categories, like zero, finite or infinite)

PRIMARY SPECIES EQUATION = (TC-((POWER(TC,(1/D))-D)^D)+1)

SPECIES EQUATION - 2 = (((TC-((POWER(TC,(1/D))-D)^D)/4)+1)

SPECIES EQUATION - 1 = (((TC-((POWER(TC,(1/D))-D)^D)/2)+1)

SPECIES EQUATION +1 = ((TC-((POWER(TC,(1/D))-D)^D)+1)*2)

SPECIES EQUATION + 2 = ((TC-((POWER(TC,(1/D))-D)^D)+1)*4)

2022-04-10: THE FORGE OF CONSTANTS

CONCEPTUAL DIMENSIONS, INPUT (Example: 2)

TOTAL CATEGORIES, INPUT (Example: 25, An exclusive permutation, for example this could be done with math by making a category square permuting Neg Inf, Finite, Zero, Neg Finite, Neg Inf with the same).

PHYSICAL DIMENSIONS, (Example of output: 11) = [(Tcategories - Nroot of T) - [(Nroot of T - N) ^N]] = ((TC-(POWER(TC,(1/CD))))-((POWER(TC,(1/CD))-CD)^CD))

NUMBER OF IDEAS (Example of output: 20) = Tcategories - Nroot of T = (TC-(POWER(TC,(1/CD))))

HIGHER LEVEL---> ALTERNATE IDEAS -2 = =(((TC-(POWER(TC,(1/CD))))/4)+1)

ALTERNATE IDEAS -1 = (((TC-(POWER(TC,(1/CD))))/2)+1)

ALTERNATE IDEAS +1 =(((TC-(POWER(TC,(1/CD))))+1)*2)

LOWER LEVEL----> ALTERNATE IDEAS +2 =(((TC-(POWER(TC,(1/CD))))+1)*4)

consider restricting to squares of odd numbers

Categories which result in whole numbers:

Cats (PhysD, Ideas, Alt -1, Alt -2, Alt +1, Alt +2)

CONCEPTUAL DIMENSIONS 8

TOTAL CATEGORIES 2097152 (FYI this appears to be a 2 base 16)

PHYSICAL DIMENSIONS 2097019.415

NUMBER OF IDEAS 2097145.831

SPECIES: 2097026.583

2nd dimension

1 (-1, 0, 1, 1, 2, 4)

9 (5,6, 4, 2.5, 14, 28)

25 (11, 20, 11, 6, 42, 84) TOE

49 (17,42, 22, 11.5, 86, 172)

81 (23, 72, 37, 19, 146, 292)

121 (29, 110, 56, 28.5, 222, 444)

169 (35, 156, 79, 40, 314, 628)

225 (41, 210, 106, 53.5, 422, 844)

289 (47, 272, 137, 69, 546, 1092)

361 (53, 342, 172, 86.5, 686, 1372)

441 (59, 420, 211, 106, 842, 1684)

529 (65, 506,254,127.5,1014,2028)

625 (71,600,301,151,1202,2404)

3rd dimension

1 (8,0, 1, 1, 2, 4) coordinates

27 (24,24, 13, 7, 50, 100) key to Dims

125 (112, 120, 61, 31, 242, 484)

343 (272, 336, 169, 85, 674, 1348)

729 (504, 720, 361, 181, 1442, 2884)

1331 (808, 1320, 661, 331, 2642, 5284)

2197 (1184, 2184, 1093, 547, 4370, 8740)

3375 (1632, 3360, 1681,841,6722,13444)

4913 (2152, 4896, 2449, 1225, 9794, 19588)

6859 (2744,6840,3421,1711,13682,27364)

9261 (3408,9240,4621,2311,18482,36964)

12167 (4144,12144,6073,3037,24290,48580)

15625 (4952,15600,7801,3901,31202,62404)

4th dimension

1 (-81,0,1,1,2,4)

81 (77,78,40,20.5,158,316)

625 (619,620,311,156,1242,2484)

2401 (2313,2394,1198,599.5,4790,9580)

6561 (5927,6552,3277,1639,13106,26212)

14641 (12229,14630,7316,3658.5,29262,58524)

28561 (21987,28548,14275,7138,57098,114196)

50625 (35969,50610,25306,12653.5,101222,202444)

83521 (54943,83504,41753,20877,167010,334020)

130321 (79677,130302,65152,32576.5,260606,521212)

194481 (110939,194460,97231,48616,388922,777844)

279841 (149497,279818,139910,69955.5,559638,1119276)

390625 (196119,390600,195301,97651,781202,1562404)

2022-04-10: ALIEN INTELLIGENCES

Consider: 0.2640625 **INTELLIGENCE RELATIVE TO THE NUMBER OF
PHYSICAL DIMENSIONS & TOE CATEGORIES**
"ALIEN I.Q."

D	TCat	Intelligence		D	TCat	Intelligence	
2	1	negligible		4	1	negligible	
2	9	1.2	PERFECT 4 IDEAS	4	81	1.013	PERFECT 40 IDEAS
2	25	1.8181		4	625	1	
2	49	2.47	PERFECT 22 IDEAS	4	2401	1.035	PERFECT 1198 IDEAS
2	81	3.13		4	6561	1.1	
2	121	3.793	PERFECT 56 IDEAS	4	14641	1.2	PERFECT 7316 IDEAS
2	169	4.457		4	28561	1.3	
2	225	5.12	PERFECT 106 IDEAS	4	50625	1.41	PERFECT 25306 IDEAS
2	289	5.787		4	83521	1.52	
2	361	6.453	PERFECT 172 IDEAS	4	130321	1.635	PERFECT 65152 IDEAS
2	441	7.119		4	194481	1.753	
2	529	7.785	PERFECT 254 IDEAS	4	279841	1.872	PERFECT 139910 IDEAS
2	625	8.45		4	390625	1.99	

D	TCat	Intelligence	
3	1	negligible	
3	27	1	
3	125	1.07	
3	343	1.235	
3	729	1.429	
3	1331	1.634	NO
3	2197	1.84	IMMEDIAT-ELY PERF-
3	3375	2.059	ECT IDEAS
3	4913	2.275	
3	6859	2.493	
3	9261	2.71	
3	12167	2.93	
3	15625	3.15	

D = CONCEPTUAL DIMENSIONS TC = MATH CATEGORIES

INTELLIGENCE = IDEAS / PHYSD

This gives number lust relative to the number of physical dimensions.

PHYSICAL DIMESIONS =
Number of Math Categories Minus Negative Dimensions then Minus The Neutral (Inner Area) = (Tcategories - Droot of T) - [(Droot of T - D) ^D]

IDEAS = Number of Math Categories Minus Negative Dimensions = (Tcategories - Nroot of T)

2022-04-27- WORK ON 'EVOLUTION OF ALL IDEAS' EXPRESSES CLASSIFICATION OF ALL MAGIC POWER.

COHERENT MAGIC (2022–04–27): 15A: MAGICAL POWER

COHERENCE (2022–04–27): 14A: SUPER-COHERENCE, 15B: COHERENT MAGIC

COHERENT PERPETUAL MOTION (2022–04–27): 13A: PERPETUAL MOTION MACHINES, 14B: COHERENT PERPETUAL MOTION, 15C: MAGICAL MACHINES

COHERENT UNIQUES (2022–04–27): 12A: UNIQUE UNIQUENESS, 13B: UNIQUE PERPETUAL MOTION, 14C: UNIQUE COHERENCE, 15D: MAGICAL UNIQUES

COHERENT CONSTANTS (2022–04–27): 11A: CONSTANT CONSTANTS, 12B: UNIQUE CONSTANTS, 13C: PERPETUAL MOTION CONSTANTS, 14D: COHERENT CONSTANTS, 15E: MAGICAL CONSTANTS

COHERENT MATHEMATICS (2022–04–27): 10A: HIGHER HIGHER MATH, 11B: CONSTANTS OF HIGHER MATH, 12C: HIGHER MATH UNIQUES, 13D: PERPETUAL MOTION MATH, 14E: HIGHER COHERENT MATH, 15F: HIGHER MAGICAL MATHEMATICS

COHERENT INTELLIGENCE (2022–04–27): 9A: INTELLIGENT INTELLIGENCE, 10B: HIGHER INTELLIGENCE OF MATHEMATICS, 11C: INTELLIGENCE CONSTANTS, 12D: UNIQUE INTELLIGENCE, 13E: PERPETUAL INTELLIGENCE, 14F: COHERENT INTELLIGENCE, 15G: HIGHER MAGICAL INTELLIGENCE

COHERENT DRUGS (2022–04–27)

8A: SUPER-DRUGS, 9B: INTELLIGENT DRUGS, 10C: CHEMISTRY OF HIGHER MATHEMATICS, 11D: CHEMICAL CONSTANTS, 12E: UNIQUE DRUGS, 13F: PERPETUAL MOTION DRUG, 14G: COHERENT DRUGS, 15H: MAGICAL DRUGS

COHERENT GENETICS (2022–04–27): 7A: SUPER-GENETICS, 8B: GENETICALLY-DELIVERED DRUGS, 9C: GENETIC INTELLIGENCE, 10D: HIGHER MATH GENETICS, 11E: GENETIC CONSTANTS, 12F: UNIQUE GENETICS, 13G: PERPETUAL GENETICS, 14H: COHERENT GENETICS, 15I: MAGICAL GENETICS

COHERENT LANGUAGES (2022–04–27): 6A: SUPER-LANGUAGES, 7B: GENETIC LANGUAGES, 8C: DRUG LANGUAGES, 9D: LINGUISTIC INTELLIGENCE, 10E: HIGHER MATH LANGUAGES, 11F: LANGUAGE CONSTANTS, 12G: UNIQUE LANGUAGE, 13H: PERPETUAL LANGUAGE, 14I: COHERENT LANGUAGE, 15J: MAGICAL LANGUAGES

COHERENT EVOLUTION (2022–04–27): 5A: META-EVOLUTION, 6B: LANGUAGE EVOLUTION, 7C: GENETIC EVOLUTION, 8D: EVOLUTIONARY DRUGS, 9E: INTELLIGENT EVOLUTION, 10F: EVOLUTIONARY HIGHER MATH, 11G: EVOLUTIONARY CONSTANTS, 12H: UNIQUE EVOLUTIONS, 13I: PERPETUAL EVOLUTION, 14J: COHERENT EVOLUTION, 15K: MAGICAL EVOLUTION

COHERENT MATERIALISM (2022–04–27): 4A: FRESH MATERIALS, 5B: NEW MATERIALS FROM EVOLUTION, 6C: NEW MATERIALS OF LANGUAGE, 7D: NEW GENETIC MATERIAL, 8E: DRUG AS NEW MATERIAL, 9F: NEW MATERIAL OF INTELLIGENCE, 10G: NEW HIGHER MATH MATERIALS, 11H: NEW MATERIAL CONSTANTS, 12I: UNIQUE NEW MATERIALS, 13J: PERPETUAL MATERIALS, 14K: COHERENT PHYSICS, 15L: MAGICAL MATERIALS

COHERENT IMMATERIALISM (2022–04–27): 3A: IMMATERIAL IMMATERIALISM, 4B: INSIGNIFICANT NEW MATERIALS, 5C: PAST EVOLUTIONS, 6D: OBSOLETE LANGUAGES, 7E: OBSOLETE GENETICS, 8F: IMMATERIALIST DRUGS, 9G: IMMATERIAL INTELLIGENCE, 10H: HIGHER MATH IMMATERIALS, 11I: IMMATERIAL CONSTANTS, 12J: UNIQUE IMMATERIALS, 13K: ABSTRACT PERPETUAL MOTION, 14L: IMMATERIAL COHERENCE, 15M: IMMATERIAL MAGICS

COHERENT APPLICATIONS (2022–04–27): 2B: APPLIED VIRTUAL REALITY, 3B: NEGATIVISTIC APPLICATIONS, 4C: NEW PHYSICAL APPLICATIONS, 5D: EVOLUTIONARY APPLICATIONS, 6E: APPLICATIONIST LANGUAGES, 7F: GENETIC APPLICATIONS, 8G: DRUG APPLICATIONS, 9H: INTELLIGENT APPLICATIONS, 10I: HIGHER MATH APPLICATIONS, 11J: APPLICATIONIST CONSTANTS, 12K: UNIQUE APPLICATIONS, 13L: PERPETUAL MOTION APPLICATIONS, 14M: COHERENT APPLICATIONS, 15N: MAGICAL APPLICATIONS

COHERENT VIRTUAL REALITY (2022–04–27): 1A: CERTAINTY AND UNCERTAINTY (VIRTUAL REALITY), 2B: APPLIED VIRTUAL REALITY, 3C: NEGATIVE REALITY, 4D: NEW PHYSICS OF VIRTUAL REALITY, 5E: VIRTUAL REALITY EVOLUTION, 6F: VIRTUAL REALITY LANGUAGES, 7G: VIRTUAL REALITY GENETICS, 8H: VIRTUAL REALITY DRUGS, 9I: VIRTUAL REALITY INTELLIGENCE, 10J: VIRTUAL REALITY OF HIGHER MATH, 11K: VIRTUAL REALITY CONSTANTS, 12L: UNIQUE SCENARIOS, 13M: VIRTUAL PERPETUAL MOTION, 14N: COHERENT VIRTUAL REALITY, 15O: VIRTUAL REALITY MAGIC

2022-04-29: Marie Antoinette's spell: 'Volar, Ayudar' meaning something like flight assistant, is kept secret until this time, under the belief it may be the last of Guo's luck.

2022-05-02: EVOLUTION OF ALL IDEAS, PROJECT VERSION

Level 1: [ENERGY NOT LANGUAGE?]

1A: CERTAINTY AND UNCERTAINTY (VIRTUAL REALITY)

- 0 and -0. [Integration of -0 as virtual reality 2022–05–02]

...

- ABOVE: Dimension: -4 and -5

Level 2: [MOVEMENTS / POLITICS / UNFAIRNESS SECRET?]

2A: METAPHYSICAL APPLICATIONS

- System 1. Gods. Movements.

2B: APPLIED VIRTUAL REALITY

- System 2. Shaders. Categories.

...

- ABOVE: Dimension: -3 and -2

Level 3: [REALISM?]

3A: IMMATERIAL IMMATERIALISM: IRRATIONALITY

- Ex nihilo.
- Ex nihilism.
- Ex nihilisthmus.
- Ex nihilation.
- Recycling cultures.
- Imaginary substances.

3B: NEGATIVISTIC APPLICATIONS: IRRATIONALITY (OFFENSE)

- Warning signs.
- Failsafe.
- Jet pack.
- Utter random chaos.

3C: NEGATIVE REALITY: IRRATIONALITY

- Bad or good.
- Double-negative.
- Smart.
- Cognition.

...

- ABOVE: Dimension: - 1

Level 4: [LIMITS? SELECTIONS?]

4A: FRESH MATERIALS: NEUTRAL ADVANTAGE

Energy

- An amount of potential niftiness.

Immortality

- From modified luck.

Universals

- Abstract immortality.

Exceptions

- Rarity / commonness.

Space-Time

- Time-travel from temporal waves, 'buying time'.

Bad Luck Magic

- Bad luck applied to problems produces psychic responses, or good fortune applied to perfect situations though with a devilish reputation (e.g. outputting bad luck though sometimes in a trivial sense if someone seeks meaning).

Logic

- It is thought.

Emotions

- Emotions apparently scale to immortality drugs.

—List of reduced (in this case coherent for our universe) 'barriers' deconstructed into technologies with explanations above, On Capturing the 5 Elements

4B: INSIGNIFICANT NEW MATERIALS: NEUTRAL ADVANTAGE

- Pain.
- Death.
- Meaninglessness.
- Irrelevance.
- Incoherence.
- Arbitrariness.
- Randomness.
- Insignificance.
- Baselessness.
- Confusion.
- Error.
- Mistakes.
- Forgetfulness.
- Annoyance.

4C: NEW PHYSICAL APPLICATIONS: NEUTRAL ADVANTAGE

- Extensions / Accumulations.
- Combinations / Permutations.
- Memories / Information.
- Enjoyment / Fantasy.

4D: NEW PHYSICS OF VIRTUAL REALITY: NEUTRAL ADVANTAGE

- Metaphysical semantics.

...

- ABOVE: Dimension: 0 and 1

...

Level 5: [T.O.E.?]

5A: META-EVOLUTION (NEUTRAL)

- Superior evolution.
- Hyper-evolution.
- Evolution praecox.

5B: NEW MATERIALS FROM EVOLUTION (NEUTRAL)

- Architecture:
  - Symmetry / Asymmetry.
  - Organic / Concrete.
  - Centralized / Decentralized.
  - Public Space / Transition space.
- Engineering:
  - Physics.
  - Machine tools.

5C: PAST EVOLUTIONS (NEUTRAL)

- Evolution typically occurs over very long time-periods. Calling results definite at any one given time is a deception.

5D: EVOLUTIONARY APPLICATIONS (NEUTRAL)

- Bones: Casting the bones.
- Shadows: The shadowland
- Pelts: The Peltland.
- The Mountains: The Headlands.
- The King: The Kingdom.
- The Golden Age: The Fortunate Man.
- Pinnacles: Apex Flow (...)

5E: VIRTUAL REALITY EVOLUTION (NEUTRAL)

- Cat's Cradle --> Solution to problems.
- Soul on a Stick --> Formula for souls.
- Self-Beating Drum --> Perpetual motion machines.
- Xes and O's --> Categorical knowledge.
- Q & A --> Answers to all questions.
- Suggestion Box --> Psychic powers.
- Dice --> Incoherent deduction.
- Passwords --> Theory of Everything.
- Higher Man: A valuable treasure.
- Money: A man from heaven.

- Religion: Mother and father.
- War: Hoisted up.
- Trickery: Only the gods could read this.
- Gods: Larger than life.
- Monsters: The stuff of legend.
- Philosophy: the joy of truth.
- Steel: From a mishandled note.
- Books: Blast onto the scene.
- Gunpowder: Let history begin.
- Mozart: We're passing at a clip.
- Paperclip: It's your relative.
- Einstein is slinking away.
- Simulation is looking hunky.
- Perpetual Motion: I'm stimmed, a simulagra
- The meaning of life is not mooks.

...

- ABOVE: Dimension: 0

...

Level 6: [RARITIES / COLLECTIONS?]

6A: SUPER-LANGUAGES

Characteristica Universalensis

- Categories.
- Vertical = entity, value, principle, power.
- Horizontal = degree, standard, commonality, honor.
- Diagonal: judgment, energy, resources, substance.
- Organic lines: coherence, boundary, dimensions, limit.
- Systems: identities.
- Substance: quanta, bosons, spacetime, posits.
- Abstracta: complexity, efficiency, perfection, beauty
- Organon: Nature, Wisdom.
- Flags: Inflection, Incorporation, Notation, Tradition.

—On the Characteristica Universalensis (...)

6B: LANGUAGE EVOLUTION

Magic Books:

- <u>Formula for Souls</u>

6C: NEW MATERIALS OF LANGUAGE

- Over-Unity Language
    - 'And stare ope-mouthed at those chill jaws!'
    - Pick a pond past beyond, rake a lake, drop a chain, deep within, throw the pin, shatter ice, dive and swim.
    - While they were floundering I was pondering / No more wandering through the dark tunnels of grim determination / For NO / It is time to grow in a thousanrd-folded folds / For which we need an Infinite Fuel!

6D: OBSOLETE LANGUAGES

- Reminder languages.
- Automatic languages.
- Meaningless nuances.
- Filligree perfect languages.

6E: APPLICATIONIST LANGUAGES

- Sublime Key Languages.
- Context Field Languages.
- Associative Languages.
- Computer Languages.

6F: VIRTUAL REALITY LANGUAGES

- Faded Rustic Languages.
- Decorative Languages.
- Performance Languages.
- Interface Languages.

...

- ABOVE: Dimension: 2

...

Level 7: [INSANITIES / METAPHYSICS / GENERAL PROBLEMS?]

7A: SUPER-GENETICS (NEUTRALITY IMMORTALITY)

- Aliens.
- Gods.
- World leaders.
- Historical geniuses.
- Folk heroes.
- Consumers.

7B: GENETIC LANGUAGES (NEUTRALITY IMMORTALITY)

- Surface cultures.

7C: GENETIC EVOLUTION (NEUTRALITY IMMORTALITY)

- Phenomenal experiences of environment.

7D: NEW GENETIC MATERIAL (NEUTRALITY IMMORTALITY)

- Given evolution, new efficient species Requires new basic systems.

7E: OBSOLETE GENETICS (NEUTRALITY IMMORTALITY)

- You have a paradigm, then you do something just for demonstration.

7F: GENETIC APPLICATIONS (NEUTRALITY IMMORTALITY)

- [The] primary problem is having the wrong nature.
- The second problem is having the wrong adaptation.
- The third problem is if one doesn't have physical means to pleasure and wealth.
- And, the fourth problem is if one doesn't have intelligence enough to find wisdom and meaning. —Practical Perfections (...)

7G: VIRTUAL REALITY GENETICS (NEUTRALITY IMMORTALITY)

- Enhancement.

...

- ABOVE: Dimension: 0 and 3

...

Level 8: [DIFFERENCES / LUXURIES, SPECIFIC PROBLEMS?]

8A: SUPER-DRUGS (NEUTRAL)

- Real-life: pennicilin (reduces infections).
- Real life: Jiaogulan (Eastern herb that may extend life).
- Real life: resperidone (relatively good treatment for schizophrenia).

8B: GENETICALLY-DELIVERED DRUGS (NEUTRAL)

- Sugar-binding / stomach-delivered.
- Infusion.
- Immunity-delivered.
- Neurological.

8C: DRUG LANGUAGES (NEUTRAL)

- Gestalt compromise (abstraction versus pleasure, but not both).

8D: EVOLUTIONARY DRUGS (NEUTRAL)

- Something to do with evoking "15 April, 2018". Evolutionary drugs mentioned in the writing 'Evolving into a Great Dragon From a Koi Fish - Chapter 227' (by May 2022).

8E: DRUG AS NEW MATERIAL (NEUTRAL)

- Something related to Dec 6, 2018. A magical day. Magical gifts. On this day, one seems to get one wish, no matter how powerful it is.

8F: IMMATERIALIST DRUGS (NEUTRAL)

- February 20, 2021 Associated with this day, someone may sometimes become undead or lighter than air.

8G: DRUG APPLICATIONS (NEUTRAL)

Unification is cognitive bias.

Division is just sensation.

[Like little drug atoms opening up].

—If all things have attributes, and all things share the attribute of existence, and no two things could share the same attributes, does that mean that all things are forms of one existence?

8H: VIRTUAL REALITY DRUGS (NEUTRAL)

- Madness, pain, etc might be drugs in virtual reality without having negative effects. The reverse psychology is used by video game developers to make drugs seem really serious even in a video game.

...

- ABOVE: Dimension: 0

...

Level 9: [IMMORTALITY/ PSEUDO-PROBLEMS?]

9A: INTELLIGENT INTELLIGENCE (GENIUS)

- Paroxysm.
- Synergasm.

9B: INTELLIGENT DRUGS (GENIUS)

- Work of art evoking the Derivative

HYPER-CUBISM   Nov 2014   Nathan Coppedge

—How can I learn calculus purely through visuals? (...)

9C: GENETIC INTELLIGENCE (GENIUS)

(1) Do they want to do physical work for pay?

(2) Do they qualify for professional training like being a computer programmer or a nurse?

(3) Are they creative or philosophical, where they might work independently for a small amount of money, like receiving charity and doing what they want that might make society more interesting and complex?

(4) Do they qualify for a leadership role?

(5) Are they all around just fun people to be around or somehow reassuring or helpful in some way?

(6) Are they drug addicts who pay money into the system?

(7) Are they just helpful in a pinch, like helping a president drive to Maryland?

(8) Are they qualified to be in the military?

(9) Are they qualified to be an academic?

(10) Maybe they are not fun, but are very attractive or have good genes?

(11) Maybe they organize people or are useful for communication or languages.

9D: LINGUISTIC INTELLIGENCE (GENIUS)

If something were not a category, it would have nothing.

If something could not stand, it would have a powerful base.

If something could not spread out, it would have length.

If something were incapable, it would swim in a soup.

If something were not alive, it could still be classified.

If something were not a system, it could still be called one.

If something had no substance, it would not exist.

If something was not abstract, it would exist.

If something was not organized, it would be a part of nature.

If something were not flagged, it would be noted.

Thus, everything that speaks a language must have one of these things, the first or the second.

And, so, everything that is missing one language is speaking another.

In the broadest sense, if we do not adhere to one modality, another modality applies.

9E: INTELLIGENT EVOLUTION (GENIUS)

HISTORY OF IDEAS PAPER

START ANYWHERE, ARRANGE CHRONOLOGICALLY

These refer to rough dates of each invention as a science.

Technological Complex is	Technological Complex is
Technological Simple is	Technological Simple is
Artistic Simple is	Artistic Simple is
Artistic Complex is	Artistic Complex is
Cosmological Complex is	Cosmological Complex is
Cosmological Simple is	Cosmological Simple is
Physical Simple is	Physical Simple is
Physical Complex is	Physical Complex is
A New Concept is	A New Concept is
Technological Complex is	Technological Complex is
Technological Simple is	Technological Simple is
Artistic Simple is	Artistic Simple is
Artistic Complex is	Artistic Complex is
Cosmological Complex is	Cosmological Complex is
Cosmological Simple is	Cosmological Simple is
Physical Simple is	Physical Simple is
Physical Complex is	Physical Complex is
A New Concept is	A New Concept is

PROOF: (1)No Nc --> Limited complexity (brain science), Limited complexity - -> No Tc (technology), No Nc - -> No Tc (hypothetical syllogism), Nc --> Tc (negation or double-negation), Nc, Tc (2)Tc --> Ts(Ockham) else No Tc., Tc, therefore Ts (3)All Ts (includes As), Sufficient Ts therefore sufficient As(4) Ts --> As, (c, s) measure same thing., Tc --> Ac, Tc, Ac(5) Ac is a symbol for Cc, A symbol is a description., Ac --> Description Cc (Substitution)., Description Cc equivalent to Cc (Descriptive materialism), Ac, Cc (6)Ac --> Description Cc, (c,s) measure same thing., As --> Description Cs, As, Cs (Descriptive materialism). (7) Cs = Ps Existential Tautology., Ps (8) Cc, Cs, Ps, (c, s) measure same thing., Pc (combination) (9)No Nc - -> No Tc (from 1), Tc (from 1) supported by Pc (from 8), Nc (modus tollens and negation applied twice).

9F: NEW MATERIAL OF INTELLIGENCE (GENIUS)

Perpetual motion brain, Enchanter's brain, Historical brain, Magic brain, Eclectic brain, Occult scientist brain. —The Eternal Golden Brain (...)

9G: IMMATERIAL INTELLIGENCE (GENIUS)

* Intelligence concerning what is not significant: [The number 160 (not IQ) is associated with meaninglessness].

9H: INTELLIGENT APPLICATIONS (GENIUS)

* Coherence, Trees, Modules, Subsets.

9I: VIRTUAL REALITY INTELLIGENCE (GENIUS)

* The size of the cranium, primarily. 'Look at the size of his cranium'. A real life person knows some people with small heads have impressive craniums.

...

* ABOVE: Dimension: 4

...

Level 10: [PERPETUAL MOTION / FLAWS?]

10A: HIGHER HIGHER MATH (NEUTRAL RARE)

* The Special Value Theorem: [1 (Efficiency) + 0.5 (Difference)] - D

10B: HIGHER INTELLIGENCE OF MATHEMATICS (NEUTRAL RARE)

* Genius Number: 1 /(((Min Eff+1 - (Max Eff / 2)+1)/ Efficiency) + 1)

10C: CHEMISTRY OF HIGHER MATHEMATICS (NEUTRAL RARE)

* Processes people go through.

10D: HIGHER MATH GENETICS (NEUTRAL RARE)

* SPECIES EQUATION: (TC-((POWER(TC,(1/D))-D)^D)+1)
* SPECIES EQUATION - 2 = (((TC-((POWER(TC,(1/D))-D)^D)/4)+1)
* SPECIES EQUATION - 1 = (((TC-((POWER(TC,(1/D))-D)^D)/2)+1)
* SPECIES EQUATION +1 = ((TC-((POWER(TC,(1/D))-D)^D)+1)*2)
* SPECIES EQUATION + 2 = ((TC-((POWER(TC,(1/D))-D)^D)+1)*4)

10E: HIGHER MATH LANGUAGES (NEUTRAL RARE)

- Ifs(Dimensions<=0,"0",Dimensions<4,(1.585*1.09^(Dimensions-2)),Dimensions=4,(1.585*1.09^(Dimensions-2)+1.09^(Dimensions-3)),Dimensions>4,(1.585*1.09^(Dimensions-2+N(1)+1.09^(Dimensions-3+N(1))))) [Thought to be effective in all higher dimensions]

10F: EVOLUTIONARY HIGHER MATH (NEUTRAL RARE)

- Patience, conserve strength.

10G: NEW HIGHER MATH MATERIALS (NEUTRAL RARE)

- Advantageous, sexy, state of the art.

10H: HIGHER MATH IMMATERIALS (NEUTRAL RARE)

- Quantum Observed: 2 / Avg Speed = Observed (Theoretical)
- Quantum Detected: [Sq rt of 0.5 (Time)] / Avg Speed = Detected
- Quantum Rules: The first observer aims to refute. The second observer acts passively. The first particle responds quickly. The last particle is a slave.

10I: HIGHER MATH APPLICATIONS (NEUTRAL RARE)

- Universe Probability: ABS((2/(D+1E-13))-(Results/(OU+(D^Results)-(Difference+5-1.00000001))))
- Difference >9.5 anywhere, Universe Expands.
- Dimensions = # Forces + # Antiforces.
- OU of 0.5 corresponds with gravity.
- OU of - 0.5 corresponds with buoyancy.
- Antiforce Min: (((D+2)/2)-0.5)
- Antiforce Max: ((D+2)/2
- Antiforce Norm: (AntiforceMax+AntiforceMin)/2

10J: VIRTUAL REALITY OF HIGHER MATH (NEUTRAL RARE)

- Intractable, unsolvable, genius solution, etc.

...

- ABOVE: Dimension: 0 and 5

...

Level 11: (CRITICAL DERIGATIVE) [LITERALS / LITERAL = LANGUAGE?]

11A: CONSTANT CONSTANTS (NEUTRAL)

- [0].

11B: CONSTANTS OF HIGHER MATH (NEUTRAL)

- Derigative = Diagrams.

11C: INTELLIGENCE CONSTANTS (NEUTRAL)

- NUMBER OF IDEAS (Example of output: 20) = Tcategories - Nroot of T = (TC-(POWER(TC,(1/CD))))
- ALTERNATE IDEAS -2 = =(((TC-(POWER(TC,(1/CD))))/4)+1)
- ALTERNATE IDEAS -1 = (((TC-(POWER(TC,(1/CD))))/2)+1)
- ALTERNATE IDEAS +1 =(((TC-(POWER(TC,(1/CD))))+1)*2)
- ALTERNATE IDEAS +2 =(((TC-(POWER(TC,(1/CD))))+1)*4)

11D: CHEMICAL CONSTANTS (NEUTRAL)

(Reverse-engineered from Genetic Constants):

- Contents.
- Iterations / lengths.
- Modes.
- Programs.
- Leaderboards.

11E: GENETIC CONSTANTS (NEUTRAL)

- Edits.
- Mediums.
- Agents.
- Networks.
- Organizations.

11F: LANGUAGE CONSTANTS (NEUTRAL)

- In excel, given as:
  =ifs(Dimensions<=0,"0",Dimensions<4,(1.585*1.09^(Dimensions-2)),Dimensions=4,(1.585*1.09^(Dimensions-2)+1.09^(Dimensions-3)),Dimensions>4,(1.585*1.09^(Dimensions-2+N(1)+1.09^(Dimensions-3+N(1)))))) [Thought to be effective in all higher dimensions]
- 2nd dimension: 1.585
- 3rd dimension: 1.72765

- 4th dimension: 2.9731385

11G: EVOLUTIONARY CONSTANTS (NEUTRAL)

FUNDAMENTAL ARGUMENT OF ATTRIBUTES

* **Continuations** are necessary to describe dimensions.

* **Continuations** depend on continuing.

* **Dimension x + 2 must not return to x, and dimension x - 2 must not return to x.**

***The resulting combinations are**
TITLE, attributes: (exclude 0 dimensions)
Title - ((SQRT TC - 1) / 2) Title + ((SQRT TC -1)/2)
Or, with TC = 25, D, attributes: D - 2, D + 2

11H: NEW MATERIAL CONSTANTS (NEUTRAL)

- Hydrogen, Helium, Lithium, Beryllium, Boron, Carbon, Nitrogen, Oxygen, Fluorine, Neon, Sodium, Magnesium, Aluminum, Silicon, Phosphorous, Sulfur, Chlorine, Argon, Potassium, Calcium, Scandium, Titanium, Vanadium, Chromium, Manganese, Iron, Cobalt, Nickel, Copper, Zink, Gallium, Germanium, Arsenic, Selenium, Bromine, Krypton, Rubidium, Strontium, Yttrium, Zirconium, Niobium, Molybdenum, Technetium, Ruthenium, Rhodium, Palladium, Silver, Cadmium, Indium, Tin, Antimony, Tellurium, Iodine, Xenon, Cesium, Barium, Lanthanum, Cerium, Proseodymium, Neodymium, Prometheum, Samarium, Europium, Gadalenium, Terbium, Dysprosium, Holmium, Erbium, Thulium, Ytterbium, Lutetium, Hafnium, Tantalum, Tungsten, Rhenium, Osmium, Iridium, Platinum, Gold, Mercury, Soulless element, Lead, Bismuth, Polonium, Astatine, Radon, Francium, Radium, Actinium, Thorium, Protactinium, Uranium, Neptunium,

Plutonium, Americium, Curium, Berkelium, Californium, Einsteinium, Fermium, Mendelevium, Nobelium, Lawrencium, Rutherfordium, Dubnium, Seborgium, Bohrium, Hassium, Meitnerium, Dermstadtium, Rontgenium, Copernicium, Nihonium, Flarovium, Mascovium, Livermorium, Tennessine, Ogynessan.

11I: IMMATERIAL CONSTANTS (NEUTRAL)

- Conceptual invisibility involves evoking: -31/32 energy (or minus 0.96875).

11J: APPLICATIONIST CONSTANTS (NEUTRAL)

- Below Animal Mode: Pain.
- Animal Mode: Exaggeration.
- Real Mode: Rationalism.
- Posthuman Mode: Perfection.

11K: VIRTUAL REALITY CONSTANTS (NEUTRAL)

- Cost, maintenance, upkeep, keeping up appearances, a little updating and maintenance, supply-cost, etc.

...

- ABOVE: Dimension: 0

Level 12: (CRITICAL CORE) [CATEGORIES?]

12A: UNIQUE UNIQUENESS (LOWER ATTRIBUTES)

- Wish-principles.

12B: UNIQUE CONSTANTS (LOWER ATTRIBUTES)

- Magic number 42.

12C: HIGHER MATH UNIQUES (LOWER ATTRIBUTES)

- Infinity, Pi, Euler's constant, Planck's constant, Avogadro's Number, etc.

12D: UNIQUE INTELLIGENCE (LOWER ATTRIBUTES)

How to be More Advanced than I Think:

- The example case is transcendent.
- The better case is less transcendent.
- We can apply a better standard to the better case.

- The better case is more parsimonious given the standard is better or given there is no alternative, so the better case transcends transcendence.
- The better case is more advanced than thinking.

12E: UNIQUE DRUGS (LOWER ATTRIBUTES)

13. Have Fun—I now think I have had fun, but not often enough. Usually lasts less than 2 seconds unless mirth counts.

17. Live the way I wish. Recompspective wizard.

18. Find the sweet mind. Needs consistency.

Aentropy: Think of it, humans are the locus of Aentropy: Insanity Wave, Clear Wave, Impossibility Wave (—2022–01–16)

12F: UNIQUE GENETICS (LOWER ATTRIBUTES)

- Source Genetics.
- Characteristic Genetics.
- Perfectly Genius Genetics.
- Popular Genetics.
- Winning Genetics.
- Strategic Genetics.
- Universal Genetics.

12G: UNIQUE LANGUAGE (LOWER ATTRIBUTES)

- English, Chinese.

12H: UNIQUE EVOLUTIONS (LOWER ATTRIBUTES)

- Reality (divine film).
- Life.
- Consciousness.
- Imagination.
- Inventions.
- Perpetual emotion, universal ideas, perfect diagram, rare items, infinite attributes, immortal machines, universal theory, infinite system, complex complexity.

12I: UNIQUE NEW MATERIALS (LOWER ATTRIBUTES)

- Gas.
- Liquid.
- Solid.

- Hard.
- Soft.
- Textured.
- Shiny.
- Reflective.
- Translucent.
- Patterned.
- Camouflage.
- Replica / imitation / copy.
- Repetition / system.
- Oily / organic.
- Electronic / robotic.
- Concealed / fake.
- Genetic / state-of-the-art.
- Nanomaterials.

12J: UNIQUE IMMATERIALS (LOWER ATTRIBUTES)

- 25-C: Neutrality.
- 25-C: Philosophy.
- 25-C: Psychology.
- 25-C: Logic.
- 25-C: Flavoring.
- 25-C: Reality / Unreality.

12K: UNIQUE APPLICATIONS (LOWER ATTRIBUTES)

- Granting wishes, spiritual exercise.

12L: UNIQUE SCENARIOS (LOWER ATTRIBUTES)

- Brainscape, Catamaran, Psychic scenarios, Hills and caves and land. Legends. Storied building. Stories land.

...

- ABOVE: Dimension: 6

...

Level 13: [ADVANTAGES / EDUCATION?]

13A: PERPETUAL MOTION MACHINES (MEANINGFUL INVENTIONS)

Vertical Wheels, Horizontal Wheels, Brownian Motors, Difference Modules, Pendulums, Horizontal Levers, Vertical Levers, Modular Levers, Magnets, Water Machines, Rube Goldberg Devices... Escher Machine, Modularity Solution: Next: Increase amount of counterweight, increase ball....

...

13B: UNIQUE PERPETUAL MOTION (MEANINGFUL INVENTIONS)

- Universe.
- M.C. Escher perpetual motion.
- Cold fusion.

13C: PERPETUAL MOTION CONSTANTS (MEANINGFUL INVENTIONS)

- < 150% Over-Unity for land devices not using buoyancy.
- < 250% Over-Unity for flying devices making maximum known use of buoyancy.

13D: PERPETUAL MOTION MATH (MEANINGFUL INVENTIONS)

- Min Results = (Max Eff / 2) + Diff
- Max Results = Min Eff + Diff
- Min Eff = Results - Diff
- Max Eff = (Min Results - Diff) X 2
- Over-Unity = ((Max Results - Min Results) / (Max Eff)) + Diff X 100 (%)
- Proportion of Smaller Unit = 1X

PERPETUAL MOTION PAPER
USED FOR CALCULATING WORKING PERPETUAL MOTION PROPERTIES

PERPETUAL MOTION CHEATSHEET

v 1

>H	>V
MECHANICS	
COMBOS	1-PRINCIPLE
GRAVITY	CYCLICAL
FUEL	I / O
UNIDIR	DUAL-DIR
STEMS	MOBILE U
SUBCYCLES OPTIONAL	
TENSILE	BENDY
L. STRUCT	H. STRUCT

SOMETIMES...

LEVER	WHEEL ONLY
HEAVY CW	LIGHT CW
SYMMETRIC	

[nathan coppedge @ Quora.com]

HORIZONTAL LEVERAGE DEVICES

MAX LEVERAGE = _____

MIN LEVERAGE = _____

MAX COUNTERWEIGHT MASS = MIN LVG + 1 = _____

MIN COUNTERWEIGHT MASS = (MAX LVG / 2) + 1 _____

ADDITIONAL LONG-END MASS = 1 (CONSTANT)

OVER-UNITY =

[(MAX CTRWEIGHT − MIN CTRWEIGHT) / MAX LVG] + 1 MASS X 100

= _____% OU + 100 IF FLYING

UNUSUAL CASES (FOR ESCHER PUT EFF = 1.25)

AMOUNT OF EFFICIENCY (MASS X LEVERAGE) _____

(X) GRADIENT IN PERCENT DEGREES (0 -1) _____

= _____ = E

AMOUNT OF RESISTANCE (MASS X LEVERAGE) _____

(X) GRADIENT IN PERCENT DEGREES (0 - 1) _____

= _____ = R

(E / R) X 100 = _____% OU

13E: PERPETUAL INTELLIGENCE (MEANINGFUL INVENTIONS)

- Relevance.
- Law of survival.
- Meta-Functions.
- Fluent Paradigms.

13F: PERPETUAL MOTION DRUG (MEANINGFUL INVENTIONS)

- The Bitter Herb.
- Healthy Drinks.
- Stone Soup.
- Inexorable Sublime Atavism.
- The Golden Fruit.

13G: PERPETUAL GENETICS (MEANINGFUL INVENTIONS)

- Perpetual Planet.
- Perpetual Platform.
- Immortality Genes.
- Divine Variation.
- Spiritual Landscape.
- Immortal Planet.
- Divine Landscape.
- Divine Results.
- Spiritual Universe.
- The Good Power.
- Meaningful Momentum (shortcut).

13H: PERPETUAL LANGUAGE (MEANINGFUL INVENTIONS)

- Perpetual motion is an important part of analysis...!

13I: PERPETUAL EVOLUTION (MEANINGFUL INVENTIONS)

- If manufacturing and God go together, and factories and perpetual motion go together, and manufacturing and factories go together, then perpetual motion and God might be the same thing.

13J: PERPETUAL MATERIALS (MEANINGFUL INVENTIONS)

- Virtual Diamonds.
- Marauder's maps.
- Eternal Depth.
- Butterfly dreams.

13K: ABSTRACT PERPETUAL MOTION (MEANINGFUL INVENTIONS)

- The Oroboros.
- Turn Key.
- The Myth of Sisyphus.
- The Robot in the Labyrinth.
- A Midsummer Night's Dream / The Enchanted Tower.

13L: PERPETUAL MOTION APPLICATIONS (MEANINGFUL INVENTIONS)

- Energy.
- Mechanics.
- Free Money.
- Optimism.
- Magic Luck.

13M: VIRTUAL PERPETUAL MOTION (MEANINGFUL INVENTIONS)

- Mobius strip video.

...

- ABOVE: Dimension: 7 and 8

...

Level 14: [ATTRIBUTES?]

14A: SUPER-COHERENCE (TOE TERRITORY)

- Coherent justice.
- Inexorable values.
- Luxury consciousness.

14B: COHERENT PERPETUAL MOTION (TOE TERRITORY)

- Perpetual motion soul.
- Hyper-soul.
- Double-coherent soul.

14C: UNIQUE COHERENCE (TOE TERRITORY)

- TOE: Results >= Efficiency* + Difference, where Efficiency sums to < 1 when topic is acted on, and > 1 when topic is acting, and Difference equals a whole number value from the Function Spectrum (differences of 100% net mechanical energy).
- The Inventor archetype.
- Universal substances.
- Timeless medium.

14D: COHERENT CONSTANTS (TOE TERRITORY)

Which amounts to meaning (5/32). [11-d] Sq rt of 25 /32

Which amounts to sublimism (15/17). [10-d] $15 \wedge 1 / 17$

Which amounts to meaningful systems (25/32). [9-d] $25^1 / 32$

Which amounts to philosophical technology (225/17). [8-d] $15^2 / 17$

Which amounts to preferences and dimensional worlds (625/32). [7-d] $25^2 / 32$

—Constant Calculus (...)

14E: HIGHER COHERENT MATH (TOE TERRITORY)

- Disintegral = Eff - Difference
- Antitheory = Difference - Eff

14F: COHERENT INTELLIGENCE (TOE TERRITORY)

GREAT PHILOSOPHY HISTORICAL MODEL BY NATHAN COPPEDGE

What is obvious? [input] Opposite of obvious? [input]

What is trivial in this time? [input]

What is the better 2-step of [trivial]? WISE ANSWER? [input]

What is most required for [trivial]??? You will find it is [WISE ANSWER]

PRIMARY INVENTION [WISE ANSWER] That wishes for [trivial]

Philosopher is remembered as studying [Opposite of obvious]

MAJOR WORK 1: [Opposite of obvious] application of [WISE ANSWER].

MAJOR WORK 2: Theory missing [trivial]

MAJOR WORK 3: In more than one way [trivial] is [obvious]

MAJOR WORK 4: [trivial] is also [opposite of obvious]

MAJOR WORK 5: [obvious] IT IS... BUT IT IS ALSO [opposite of obvious]

MAJOR WORK 6: Variations on concepts of [trivial]

MAJOR WORK 7: Theories about theory missing [trivial]

MAJOR WORK 8: [Opp of obvious] is missing something!

MAJOR WORK 9: Not [Obvious] with [Wise answer]

MAJOR WORK 10: [Wise answer] is great

MAJOR WORK 11: Wishing for [Trivial] is not [Obvious]

MAJOR WORK 12: What is not [Obvious] is [Wise answer]

MAJOR WORK 13: [Trivial] is missing, a theory missing [Trivial]

MAJOR WORK 14: A theory of [Trivial] is not a theory

MAJOR WORK 15: [Trivial] beyond [Trivial] beyond [Trivial]

MAJOR WORK 16: Beyond [Trivial] IS [Opp of Obvious]

MAJOR WORK 17: Paradoxical [Opp of Obvious]

MAJOR WORK 18: [Trivial] IS paradoxical

MAJOR WORK 19: Paradoxical [Obvious]

MAJOR WORK 20: [Wise answer] transcends reality

14G: COHERENT DRUGS (TOE TERRITORY)

Advanced Amulet method:

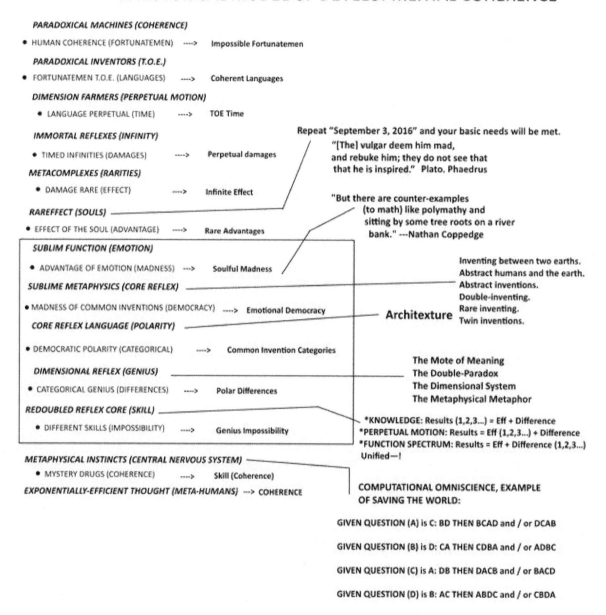

A HISTORICAL MODEL OF DEVELOPMENTAL COHERENCE

PARADOXICAL MACHINES (COHERENCE)

- HUMAN COHERENCE (FORTUNATEMEN) ----> Impossible Fortunatemen

PARADOXICAL INVENTORS (T.O.E.)

- FORTUNATEMEN T.O.E. (LANGUAGES) ----> Coherent Languages

DIMENSION FARMERS (PERPETUAL MOTION)

- LANGUAGE PERPETUAL (TIME) ----> TOE Time

IMMORTAL REFLEXES (INFINITY)

- TIMED INFINITIES (DAMAGES) ----> Perpetual damages

METACOMPLEXES (RARITIES)

- DAMAGE RARE (EFFECT) ----> Infinite Effect

RAREFFECT (SOULS)

- EFFECT OF THE SOUL (ADVANTAGE) ----> Rare Advantages

Repeat "September 3, 2016" and your basic needs will be met.
"[The] vulgar deem him mad,
and rebuke him; they do not see that
that he is inspired." Plato, Phaedrus

"But there are counter-examples
(to math) like polymathy and
sitting by some tree roots on a river
bank." ---Nathan Coppedge

SUBLIM FUNCTION (EMOTION)

- ADVANTAGE OF EMOTION (MADNESS) ---> Soulful Madness

SUBLIME METAPHYSICS (CORE REFLEX)

- MADNESS OF COMMON INVENTIONS (DEMOCRACY) ----> Emotional Democracy

CORE REFLEX LANGUAGE (POLARITY)

- DEMOCRATIC POLARITY (CATEGORICAL) ----> Common Invention Categories

DIMENSIONAL REFLEX (GENIUS)

- CATEGORICAL GENIUS (DIFFERENCES) ----> Polar Differences

REDOUBLED REFLEX CORE (SKILL)

- DIFFERENT SKILLS (IMPOSSIBILITY) ----> Genius Impossibility

Inventing between two earths.
Abstract humans and the earth.
Abstract inventions.
Double-inventing.
Rare inventing.
Twin inventions.

Architexture

The Mote of Meaning
The Double-Paradox
The Dimensional System
The Metaphysical Metaphor

*KNOWLEDGE: Results (1,2,3...) = Eff + Difference
*PERPETUAL MOTION: Results = Eff (1,2,3...) + Difference
*FUNCTION SPECTRUM: Results = Eff + Difference (1,2,3...)
Unified—!

METAPHYSICAL INSTINCTS (CENTRAL NERVOUS SYSTEM)

- MYSTERY DRUGS (COHERENCE) ----> Skill (Coherence)

EXPONENTIALLY-EFFICIENT THOUGHT (META-HUMANS) ---> COHERENCE

COMPUTATIONAL OMNISCIENCE, EXAMPLE
OF SAVING THE WORLD:

GIVEN QUESTION (A) is C: BD THEN BCAD and / or DCAB

GIVEN QUESTION (B) is D: CA THEN CDBA and / or ADBC

GIVEN QUESTION (C) is A: DB THEN DACB and / or BACD

GIVEN QUESTION (D) is B: AC THEN ABDC and / or CBDA

14H: COHERENT GENETICS (TOE TERRITORY)

- Universe DNA: [BCAD or DCAB AND (CDBA or ADBC) AND DACB or BACD AND (ABDC or CBDA)] OR [BCAD or DCAB AND (ABDC or CBDA) AND DACB or BACD AND (CDBA or ADBC)]

14I: COHERENT LANGUAGE (TOE TERRITORY)

- Ifs(Dimensions<=0,"0",Dimensions<4,(1.585*1.09^(Dimensions-2)),Dimensions=4,(1.585*1.09^(Dimensions-2)+1.09^(Dimensions-3)),Dimensions>4,(1.585*1.09^(Dimensions-2+N(1)+1.09^(Dimensions-3+N(1)))))) [Thought to be effective in all higher dimensions]

14J: COHERENT EVOLUTION (TOE TERRITORY)

Category 1 is category 13 when category 0 is close-in. - -> Impossible Humans (coherence)

Category 2 is category 14 when category 1 is close-in - -> Coherent Fortunatemen (TOE)

Category 3 is category 15 when category 2 is close-in. - -> TOE Language (perpetual motion)

Category 4 is category 16 when category 3 is close-in - -> Perpetual motion time (infinity)

Category 5 is category 17 when category 4 is close-in - -> Infinite damage (rarities)

Category 6 is category 18 when category 5 is close-in - -> Rare effect (souls)

Category 7 is category 19 when category 6 is close-in - -> Soulful advantage (emotion)

Category 8 is category 20 when category 7 is close-in - -> Emotional madness (common inventions)

Category 9 is category 21 when category 8 is close-in - -> Common invention democracy (polarity)

Category 10 is category 22 when category 9 is close-in - -> Polar categories (genius)

Category 11 is category 23 when category 10 is close-in - -> Genius difference (skill)

Category 12 is category 24 when category 11 is close-in - -> Skills in mystery (drugs or nothing)

Category 13 is category 25 when category 12 is close-in - -> Drugs or nothing impossible (humans)

Category 14 is category 0 when category 13 is close-in - -> Human coherence (fortunatemen)

Category 15 is category 1 when category 14 is close-in - -> Fortunatemen TOE (languages)

Category 16 is category 2 when category 15 is close-in - -> Language perpetual (time)

Category 17 is category 3 when category 16 is close-in - -> Timed infinities (damages)

Category 18 is category 4 when category 17 is close-in - -> Damage rare (effect)

Category 19 is category 5 when category 18 is close-in - -> Effect of the soul (advantage)

Category 20 is category 6 when category 19 is close-in - -> Advantage of emotion (madness)

Category 21 is category 7 when category 20 is close-in - -> Madness of common inventions (democracy)

Category 22 is category 8 when category 21 is close-in - -> Democratic polarity (categorical)

Category 23 is category 9 when category 22 is close-in - -> Categorical genius (differences)

Category 24 is category 10 when category 23 is close-in - -> Different skills (impossibility)

Category 25 is category 11 when category 24 is close-in - -> Mystery drugs (coherence)

Category 0 is category 12 when category 25 is close-in - -> Impossible humans (TOE)

—Close-In Logic (...)

14K: COHERENT PHYSICS (TOE TERRITORY)

- PHYSICAL DIMENSIONS, (Example of output: 11) = [(Tcategories - Nroot of T) - [(Nroot of T - N) ^N]] = ((TC-(POWER(TC,(1/CD))))-((POWER(TC,(1/CD))-CD)^CD))

14L: IMMATERIAL COHERENCE (TOE TERRITORY)

- It seeemed like the funniest, most dreadful thing. For a god to disappear—poof! A bit like getting an 'A' in conjury.

14M: COHERENT APPLICATIONS (TOE TERRITORY)

T.O.E.

- KNOWLEDGE: Results (1,2,3...) = Eff + Difference
- PERPETUAL MOTION: Results = Eff (1,2,3...) + Difference
- FUNCTION SPECTRUM: Results = Eff + Difference (1,2,3...)
- Unified—!

Anti-Theory:

- Anti-Thing (1,2,3...) <= Difference - Efficiency
- Anti-Thing <= Difference (1,2,3...) - Efficiency
- Anti-Thing <= Difference - Efficiency (1,2,3...)

Efficiency:

- Efficiency (1,2,3...) >= Results – Difference
- Efficiency >= Results (1,2,3...) – Difference
- Efficiency >= Results – Difference (1,2,3...)

Anti-Efficiency:

- Anti-Efficiency (1,2,3...) <= Difference - Results
- Anti-Efficiency <= Difference (1,2,3...) - Results
- Anti-Efficiency <= Difference - Results (1,2,3...)

Difference:

- Difference (1,2,3...) >= Results – Efficiency
- Difference >= Results (1,2,3...) – Efficiency
- Difference >= Results – Efficiency (1,2,3...)

Anti-Difference:

- Anti-Difference (1,2,3...) <= Efficiency - Results
- Anti-Difference <= Efficiency (1,2,3...) - Results
- Anti-Difference <= Efficiency - Results (1,2,3...)

Forces:

- # Forces (1,2,3...) = # Dimensions - # Antiforces
- # Forces = # Dimensions (1,2,3...) - # Antiforces
- # Forces = # Dimensions - # Antiforces (1,2,3...)

Antiforces:

- \# Antiforces (1,2,3...) = \# Dimensions - \# Forces
- \# Antiforces = \# Dimensions (1,2,3...) - \# Forces
- \# Antiforces = \# Dimensions - \# Forces (1,2,3...)

Dimensions:

- \# Dimensions (1,2,3...) = \# Forces + \# Antiforces
- \# Dimensions = \# Forces (1,2,3...) + \# Antiforces
- \# Dimensions = \# Forces + \# Antiforces (1,2,3...)

Anti-Dimensions:

- \# Anti-Dimensions (1,2,3...) = \# Antiforces - \# Forces
- \# Anti-Dimensions = \# Antiforces - \# Forces (1,2,3...) +
- \# Anti-Dimensions = \# Antiforces (1,2,3...) - \# Forces

Disintegral (same as before, by De Morgan's Rule):

- WAR EQUATION: Disintegral (1,2,3...) = Efficiency – Difference
- EFFICIENCY SPECTRUM: Disintegral = Efficiency (1,2,3...) – Difference
- GENERAL AND SPECIAL TRANSLATION: Disintegral = Efficiency – Difference (1,2,3...)

Anti-Disintegral or Abstract Efficiency (Same as Antitheory, modifying the change after De Morgan's):

- Anti-Disintegral (1,2,3...) = Difference – Efficiency
- Anti-Disintegral = Difference (1,2,3...) - Efficiency
- Anti-Disintegral = Difference - Efficiency (1,2,3...)

Super-Disintegral:

- Super-Disintegral (1,2,3...) = Inf Efficiency – Inf Difference
- Super-Disintegral = Inf Efficiency (1,2,3...) – Inf Difference
- Super-Disintegral = Inf Efficiency – Inf Difference (1,2,3...)

Anti-Super-Disintegral:

- Anti-Super-Disintegral (1,2,3...) = Inf Difference – Inf Efficiency
- Anti-Super-Disintegral = Inf Difference (1,2,3...) - Inf Efficiency
- Anti-Super-Disintegral = Inf Difference - Inf Efficiency (1,2,3...)

Min Results:

- Min Results (1,2,3...) = (Max Eff / 2) + Diff
- Min Results = (Max Eff (1,2,3...) / 2) + Diff
- Min Results = (Max Eff / 2) + Diff (1,2,3...)

Max Results:

- Max Results (1,2,3...) = Min Eff + Diff
- Max Results = Min Eff (1,2,3...) + Diff
- Max Results = Min Eff + Diff (1,2,3...)

Min Efficiency:

- Min Eff (1,2,3...) = Results - Diff
- Min Eff = Results (1,2,3...) - Diff
- Min Eff = Results - Diff (1,2,3...)

Max Efficiency:

- Max Eff (1,2,3...) = (Min Results - Diff) X 2
- Max Eff = (Min Results (1,2,3...) - Diff) X 2
- Max Eff = (Min Results - Diff (1,2,3...)) X 2

Flying Max Results

- Flying Max Results (1,2,3...) = (Min Eff) + 2 Eff - 1
- Flying Max Results = (Min Eff (1,2,3...)) + 2 Eff - 1
- Flying Max Results = (Min Eff) + 2 Eff (1,2,3...) - 1

Flying Min Results

- Flying Min Results (1,2,3...) = (Max Eff / 2) + 2 Eff - 1
- Flying Min Results = (Max Eff (1,2,3...) / 2) + 2 Eff - 1
- Flying Min Results = (Max Eff / 2) + 2 Eff (1,2,3...) - 1

14N: COHERENT VIRTUAL REALITY (TOE TERRITORY)

- 16-Category Semantics.

...

- ABOVE: Dimension: 9 and 10

...

Level 15: [COHERENT WISHES?]

15A: MAGICAL POWER (DIMENSIONAL POLYMATCHIK)

- 'The Power'.

15B: COHERENT MAGIC (DIMENSIONAL POLYMATCHIK)

POSSIBILITY WAVES

- Universe 1: Coherent Wave, Wishing [10 -Dimensional]
- Universe 2: Growth Wave, TOE [9 -Dimensional]
- Universe 3: Standing Wave [8 -Dimensional]
- Universe 4: Disintegral Wave, Mathematical Integration [7 -Dimensional]
- Universe 5: Rarity Wave, Paradoxes [6-Dimensional]
- Universe 6: Souls, Psychic Source [0-Dimensional]
- Universe 7: Emotions, Product of Damages [0-Dimensional]
- Universe 8: Cores, Major Technology [0-Dimensional]
- Universe 9: Function Wave, Equal Opposites [5-Dimensional]
- Universe 10: Idea Wave, Energy Produced [4-Dimensional]
- Universe 11: Skills [0-Dimensional]
- Universe 12: Zeroverse, Drugs [0-Dimensional]
- Universe 13: Retractors, Humans [0-Dimensional]
- Universe 14: Luck Wave, Immortals [3-Dimensional]
- Universe 15: Clear Wave, Languages [2-Dimensional]
- Universe 16: Timed Events [0-Dimensional]
- Universe 17: Damages, Warping [0-Dimensional]
- Universe 18: Effects, Major Results [0-Dimensional]
- Universe 19: Communication Wave , Education [1-Dimensional]

IMPOSSIBILITY WAVES

- Universe 0: Impossibility Wave, also called Emotion Wave, Psychic Wave [11-Dimensional]
- Universe 20: Insanity Wave also called Perfection Wave, Soul Wave [-1-Dimensional]
- Universe 21: Fringe Wave also called Standardization Wave, Exception Wave [-2-Dimensional]
- Universe 22: Category Wave also called Aesthetic Wave, Beauty Wave [-3-Dimensional]
- Universe 23: Luxury Wave, also called Reality Wave, Time Wave [-4-Dimensional]
- Universe 24: Opportunity Wave, also called Creativity Wave, Working Wave [-5-Dimensional]

[Added Nov 24, 2021. See: Universe Profile]

15C: MAGICAL MACHINES (DIMENSIONAL POLYMATCHIK)

- Polymath Machines (diagram, calculus, knowledge, perpetual motion).
- Emotive Machines (Luck, simple machines, etc).
- Wave / Waveform Machines (Impossibility Wave Machines, Coherent Wave Machines, TOE Wave Machines, Exponent Machines, Energy Machines, Rarity Machines, Infinity Machines, Intelligence Machines, Luck Machines, Language Intuition Machines, Advantageous Machines, Philosophy Machines, Psychology Machines, Logic Machines, Flavor-It Machines, Illusion Machines).
- Waveform Computers (simple magic process machines, area effect machines, proper magic machines, indellible attributes, elaborate effect machines, industrial magic machines).

15D: MAGICAL UNIQUES (DIMENSIONAL POLYMATCHIK)

For example, Rumores:

Time Sword, Time Trick, Swords are Gods, Opportunity for Swords, Secret Trick is Tricky,

Time Egg, Time as A Kite, Eggs are Gods, Opportunity for Eggs, Secret as A Kite is Tricky,

Time Machines, Time Standards, Machines are Gods, Opportunity for Machines, Secret Standards is Tricky,

Time Monsters, Time Priests, Monsters are Gods, Opportunity for Monsters, Secret Priests are Tricky,

Time of Ages, Time Guides, Of Ages are Gods, Opportunity for of Ages, Secret Guides is Tricky,

Time of Pleasure, Time of Measurements, Of Pleasure are Gods, Opportunity for Pleasure, Secret of Measurements is Tricky,

Time State, Time Debauchery, States are Gods, Opportunity for States, Secret of Debauchery is Tricky,

Time Number, Time Greatness, Numbers are Gods, Opportunity for Numbers, Secret of Greatness is Tricky,

Time Time, Time Laziness, Times are Gods, Opportunity for Time, Secret of Laziness is Tricky,

Time Knowledge, Time Superficiality, Knowledges are Gods, Opportunity for Knowledge, Secret of Superficiality is Tricky

Time Yew, Time Weather, Yew are Gods, Opportunity for Yew, Secret of Weather is Tricky,

Time Abstracta, Time Prostitution, Abstract Gods, Opportunity for Abstractions, Secret of Prostitution is Tricky,

Time Exponents, Time Factors, Exponents are Gods, Opportunity for Exponents, Secret of Factors is Tricky,

Time Trumps, Time Signs, Trumps are Gods, Opportunity for Trumps, Secret of Signs is Tricky,

Time Soul. Time to Kill, Souls are Gods, Opportunity for Souls, Secret to Kill is Tricky,

Time of All Things, Time Disappointment, Of All Things are Gods, Opportunity for All Things, Secret of Disappointment is Tricky,

Time Entology, Time of Logic, Entologies are Gods, Opportunity for Entology, Secret of Logic is Tricky,

Time with Money, Time Promises, With Money are Gods, Opportunity for with Money, Secret of Promises is Tricky,

Time Reel, Time Standard, Reels are Gods, Opportunity for Reels, Secret Standard is Tricky,

Time Burgher, Time the Creeps, Burghers are Gods, Opportunity for Burghers, Secret O' the Creeps is Tricky,

Time Forever, Time Half-Life, Forevers are Gods, Opportunity for Forevers, Secret that Half-Lives are Tricky,

Time He's A Genius, Time Language, He's A Genius is Gods, Opportunity for He's A Genius, Secret of Language is Tricky,

Time on Earth, Time Nothing, On Earth is Gods, Opportunity for On Earth, Secret of Nothing is Tricky,

...

15E: MAGICAL CONSTANTS (DIMENSIONAL POLYMATCHIK)

0.13 Impossibility,

0.14 Coherence,

0.15 Theories,

0.16 Wormholes,

0.17 Disintegrals,

5.18 Rarities,

6.19 Psychics,

7.20 Emotions,

8.21 Inventions,

9.22 Diagrams,

10.23 Power Fame,

11.24 Skills VR,

12.25 Neutral Drugs

13.1 Humans, Animals Retractor Tools,

14.2 Immortality,

15.3 Languages,

16.4 Refrigerators, Ongoing effects,

17.5 Viruses, Damage, Mitigation,

18.6 Evolution, Fishing, Dying,

19.7 Groups, Weakness, Advantages,

20.8 Philosophy, Predictability,

21.9 Psychology, Indifference,

AUTHENTIC T.O.E. TECHNOLOGY

UNIVERSE 0 D = 11
X #13 IMPOSSIBILITY
RESULTS= INF,
EFF= NEG INF,
DIFF= IMPOSSIBLE

UNIVERSE 1 D = 10
#14 COHERENCE
RESULTS= INF,
EFF= NEG FIN
DIFF= RESULTS

UNIVERSE 2 D = 9
#15 THEORIES
RESULTS=INF,
EFF= 0,
DIFF= RESULTS

UNIVERSE 3 D = 8
#16 TIME-CRYSTALS, WORM-HOLES, INFINITE EVENTS
RESULTS= INF
EFF= FIN,
DIFF= RESULTS

UNIVERSE 4 D=7
#17 DISINTEGRALS
RESULTS= INF,
EFF= RESULTS
DIFF= 0

UNIVERSE 5 D = 6
X #18 RARITIES
RESULTS= FIN,
EFF= NEG INF.
DIFF = INF

UNIVERSE 6: D = 0
#19 TELEKINESIS, INVISIBILITY, TIME-TRAVEL.
RESULTS= FIN
EFF = NEG FIN
DIFF = ¬(EFF) + RESULTS

UNIVERSE 7: D = 0
#20 EMOTION
RESULTS= FIN
EFF = 0
DIFF = RESULTS

UNIVERSE 8: D = 0
#21 KNOWLEDGE, TELEPORTATION, PERPETUAL MOTION
RESULTS= FIN
EFF = FIN
DIFF = RESULTS - EFF

UNIVERSE 9 D = 5
X #22 DIAGRAMS
RESULTS= FIN,
EFF= INF,
DIFF= NEG INF

UNIVERSE 10 D = 4
#23 POWER, POPULISM
RESULTS= 0,
EFF= NEG INF,
DIFF = INF

UNIVERSE 11: D = 0
#24 SKILLS,
CONSEQUENCES
RESULTS = ZERO
EFF = NEG FIN
DIFF = FIN

UNIVERSE 12: D = 0
#25 NEUTRALITY, DRUGS, TRIVIALITY
RESULTS = ZERO
EFF = ZERO
DIFF = ZERO

UNIVERSE 13 D = 0
#1 HUMANS, ANIMALS, RETRACTING TOOLS
RESULTS = AVG ZERO
EFF = FIN
DIFF = AVG 0 + EFF

UNIVERSE 14 D = 3
#2 IMMORTALITY: USE INF ENERGY WITH INF EFF
RESULTS 0,
EFF= INF,
DIFF= NEG INF

UNIVERSE 15 D = 2
X #3 LANGUAGE, ANALOGY
RESULTS= NEG FIN,
EFF= NEG INF.
DIFF = INF

UNIVERSE 16: D = 0
#4 REFRIGERATORS, ONGOING EFFECTS
RESULTS = NEG FIN
EFF = NEG FIN
DIFF = ¬(EFF)+RESULTS

UNIVERSE 17: D = 0
#5 VIRUSES, DAMAGE, MITIGATION
RESULTS = NEG FIN
EFF = 0
DIFF = RESULTS

UNIVERSE 18: D = 0
#6 EVOLUTION, FISHING, DYING
RESULTS = NEG FIN
EFF = FIN
DIFF= NEGEFF+RESULTS

UNIVERSE 19 D = 1
#7 GROUPS, WEAKNESS, ADVANTAGES
RESULTS= NEG FIN,
X EFF= INF,
DIFF= NEG INF

UNIVERSE 20 D = NEG1
PHILOSOPHY,
#8 PREDICTABILITY
RESULTS= NEG INF,
EFF= RESULTS
DIFF= 0

UNIVERSE 21: D = NEG2
PSYCHOLOGY,
#9 INDIFFERENCE
RESULTS= NEG INF,
EFF= NEG FIN.
DIFF = RESULTS

UNIVERSE 22: D=NEG3
#10 CONSERVATISM
RESULTS= NEG INF,
EFF= 0,
DIFF= RESULTS

UNIVERSE 23: D = NEG4
#11 COMPROMISE
RESULT = NEG INF,
EFF= FIN,
DIFF= RESULTS

UNIVERSE 24 D = NEG5
X SPACE, DISTANCE, DIFFICULTY
#12
RESULTS= NEG INF,
EFF= INF,
DIFF= IMPOSSIBLE

15F: HIGHER MAGICAL MATHEMATICS (DIMENSIONAL POLYMATCHIK)

- Say a name, and it may be a number. —Mathematical Enchantment

WIZARD PAPER

FORM A SENTENCE OR TWO BETWEEN THE BLANKS:

Obvious statement _____

Then a mysterious ironic thing _____

Followed by an unexpected negative reference (to magic),

_____

followed by a certain contradiction

_____

Reproducible under Nathan Larkin Coppedge

15H: MAGICAL DRUGS (DIMENSIONAL POLYMATCHIK)

PRESCRIPTIONS FOR HAPPINESS

"And the pale moon comes"

Against Headaches: Get some sun, silently incant 'Passiv object... Boabob tree'.

Repeat "September 3, 2016" and your basic needs will be met.

Repeat "June 16, 2017" and you will find happiness.

Reproducible under Nathan Larkin Coppedge

...

PRESCRIPTIONS FOR INTELLIGENCE

Prios: End a Dark Age.

Kyron—great results for preventing negative energy.

Grow your brain: Say 'Complex cause, 4th dimension.'

Soul Protect: Don't be 'elitus' and know the word 'spiritus'.

Cure for Schizophrenia: "May 27, 2019".

Reproducible under Nathan Larkin Coppedge

...

PRESCRIPTIONS FOR LUCK

OCT 12, 2018 SURVIVAL

15 APRIL, 2018 EVOLUTION

Garden forsooth, forsooth a garden--Health spell.

Health: Avoid the barbs of magic, just cool down, and apply the phrase: "metabolic metabolism".

Fortune: Rich at heart, rich in health, rich quite well, fortunate potential.

Heh (pronounced 'hey')— secret of winning.

Juxtaphix: General spell, improve luck.

Improved Spell for Success: Say any of these that you agree with, ideally all of them:

"I am an Outsider. I am a Stoic. I am a Christian. I am a Modern Christian. I am a Traditional Rationalist. I am an Elitist Romantic. I am Modern. I am Emotional. I am a Scientist, I am Normal, I am an Authentic Radical, I am Systematic."

Reproducible under Nathan Larkin Coppedge

15I: MAGICAL GENETICS (DIMENSIONAL POLYMATCHIK)

- A servile animal.
- An everyday hero.
- A Unique Gift.
- An exceptional wizard.
- Someone abides there.
- The matter of stars.
- Common matter with no shame.
- Persistence in significance.

15J: MAGICAL LANGUAGES (DIMENSIONAL POLYMATCHIK)

- Meta-Cubism (magic cubism)

15K: MAGICAL EVOLUTION (DIMENSIONAL POLYMATCHIK)

- Forsaken independent problems.
- Trying matters.
- Intelligent matters.
- The secret formula might be helpful.
- Better luck next time.
- If I can't do it, maybe he can.
- What is not an appearance, might appear not to be.
- Languages will be enforced.

15L: MAGICAL MATERIALS (DIMENSIONAL POLYMATCHIK)

- Anti-Curses: Additional energy spinning around
- The Oroboros.
- Spooky glyph.
- 4-D waterfall.
- Seed of nirvana.
- Mote of knowledge.
- The Atavist.
- Influential.
- Time-travel.
- Transmagensis.
- ?
- The Skiller, ?, ?, ?, ?
- The Evincer, ?, ?, ?, ?
- The Metaph, ?, ?, ?, ?

15M: IMMATERIAL MAGICS (DIMENSIONAL POLYMATCHIK)

- Mind control. (ante-magic)
- Changed appearance. (anti-magic)
- Motive volitions. (ante-anti-magic)
- Elemental constructions. (ante-ante-magic)

15N: MAGICAL APPLICATIONS (DIMENSIONAL POLYMATCHIK)

- Slight of hand. Secret: move fast, and think ahead of where your hand moves. Also, create a distraction if the movement takes longer than 0.05 seconds.
- Fast movement is invisible. Moving faster than 1 body length per 0.05 seconds. Or every 0.1 to 0.5 seconds to out-of-sight (not professional advice: moving this fast might cause brain damage or other injuries).
- Balance: Centers of balance can make things easier to move and rotate. A center of balance can also be concealed, and off-balance, making one side heavier or lighter or even dangerous or fast-moving using a counterbalance.
- Dimensions can be concealed by rotating them and changing their color.
- Dimensions can be shifted through one another by collapsing or penetrating materials.
- Shapes can be inverted to make a volume larger or smaller. Reflectiveness might help with this.
- Depth can be concealed by estimation and rounding and by changing the audience's vantage point or changing conventions.
- Magic illusion.
- Magic foolery.
- Magic trickery.
- Magic appearance.
- Magic corroborators.
- Magic items.
- Magic abilities.
- Do not modify very much.
- Things cost time (this is one reason why magic seems very expensive).

15O: VIRTUAL REALITY MAGIC (DIMENSIONAL POLYMATCHIK)

- Negative theory of anything and negative negative negative zero.
- Simulation.

...

- ABOVE: Dimension: 11 —Power Levels (2022–04–27)

END OF EVOLUTION OF ALL IDEAS, PROJECT VERSION

'''

RECOMMENDED READING

OTHER TEXTS BY NATHAN COPPEDGE

'''

‴

Nathan Coppedge (b. 1982) Philosopher, Artist, Inventor, Poet and member of the international honor society for philosophers, is an abstract artist of Hyper-Cubism (sometimes said to be worth $1,000,000 or more), and is best known for his writings on philosophy and for his ingenious perpetual motion videos and diagrams. He has sold Hyper-Cubism internationally.